TEAM BUSH

Leadership Lessons from the Bush White House

DONALD F. KETTL

McGraw-Hill

New York   Chicago   San Francisco   Lisbon
London   Madrid   Mexico City   Milan   New Delhi
San Juan   Seoul   Singapore   Sydney   Toronto

Copyright © 2003 by The **McGraw-Hill** Companies, Inc. All rights reserved. Printed in the United States of America. Except as permitted under the United States Copyright Act of 1976, no part of this publication may be reproduced or distributed in any form or by any means, or stored in a data base or retrieval system, without the prior written permission of the publisher.

1 2 3 4 5 6 7 8 9 0   DOC/DOC   0 9 8 7 6 5 4 3

ISBN 0-07-141633-1

FIRST EDITION

McGraw-Hill books are available at special quantity discounts to use as premiums and sales promotions, or for use in corporate training programs. For more information, please write to the Director of Special Sales, Professional Publishing, McGraw-Hill, Two Penn Plaza, New York, NY 10121-2298. Or contact your local bookstore.

This book is printed on recycled, acid-free paper containing a minimum of 50% recycled, de-inked fiber.

Team Bush is not authorized, endorsed by, or affiliated with President George W. Bush.

Library of Congress Cataloging-in-Publication Data
Kettl, Donald F.
 Team Bush : leadership lessons from the Bush White House / by Donald F. Kettl.
     p. cm.
  ISBN 0-07-141633-1 (alk. paper)
  1. Leadership. 2. Political leadership. 3. Bush, George W. (George Walker), 1946- 4. United States—Politics and government—2001– I. Title.
  HD57.7.K49 2003
  303.3'4'092—dc21
                                                        2003000691

Contents

iii

Birth of a Commander-in-Chief

"This stuff about transformed? From my perspective, he is the same President Bush that I saw going through different issues in Texas. He's always been decisive, he's always been disciplined, he's always been really focused, he's always been a really good delegator."

—KAREN HUGHES, ON THE CHANGE IN
PRESIDENT BUSH AFTER SEPTEMBER 11

THROUGHOUT HIS CAREER as a political executive, George W. Bush has consistently exceeded expectations. Doing it once or twice might be lucky. Doing it over and over has to require real skill.

What's the secret? Bush has carefully honed a style, based on building an effective team, to make strong decisions. He doesn't try to master the complexities of decisions. Rather, he builds a team, he makes *them* master the complexities, he has them frame the issues—and *then he decides*, firmly and without second thoughts. He's ridden this style, over and over, to successes that have amazed his friends and stunned his foes.

Consider a quick scorecard. Few analysts gave him a chance of unseating Texas Governor Ann Richards in 1994, yet he beat her in the race. Political handicappers gave him slim odds for a successful gubernatorial term, but he rolled to a huge victory in 1998. He explored a presidential run, but cynics suggested he wasn't nearly smart enough to be the nation's chief executive. When he won the nomination, Democrats relished the idea of Al Gore taking him on.

One Republican insider, in fact, quietly whispered that watching Bush debate was like watching his 12-month-old daughter try to walk, "never knowing when she might fall on her face."

Bush astounded everyone by holding his own against the vice president. He rode his debate performance to a razor-thin presidential victory. When he got to Washington, insiders discounted the chance that he could accomplish anything. Most Americans doubted that Bush and congressional Democrats could put politics aside to work together. But he cobbled together enough votes to pass a big, 10-year tax cut.

Even his friends were worried about how ready he'd be to make foreign policy decisions. During the campaign, BBC News asked bluntly, "Can nice guy George Junior shed his image as a political lightweight and demonstrate that he's made of steel? Has he got what it takes for one of the most powerful jobs in the world?"

But in the aftermath of the September 11 terrorist attacks, Bush rallied the country. When he threatened the Taliban in Afghanistan, skeptics pointed to the Russians' devastating defeat in their own war with that country. Analysts warned that Bush's plan might draw the United States into another Vietnam. Bush attacked anyway. Within weeks the Taliban crumbled. Bush's approval rating soared to the highest level ever recorded.

Democrats reassured themselves with the fact that the president's party almost always loses seats in the midterm congressional elections. They thought they could keep control of the Senate and dreamed of retaking the House. Bush launched a whirlwind last-week salvo of campaigning. Republicans not only retained control of the House in 2002 but retook the Senate. Bush yet again exceeded expectations. In the process, he solidified his position. He worked to capitalize on his strength by launching an economic stimulus plan, seeking to disarm Saddam Hussein, and countering North Korea's threats to destabilize Asia.

In the aftermath of the September 11 attacks, the clear consensus was that the world had fundamentally changed. In a stirring editorial, the *New York Times* said, "It was, in fact, one of those moments in which history splits, and we define the world as 'before' and 'after.'" The sudden, awesome impact of the terrorists' attacks fundamentally transformed everything about the country and its role in the world.

If the world had changed, the striking thing is that *Bush had not*. He was the same man, with the same style, as he had been as Texas governor. He had a strong sense of confidence, a vision of what ought to be done, and a determination to do the job right. He focused on the big picture with a decide-and-delegate style torn from the pages of MBA casebooks. He didn't devise a new style to deal with the unimaginable catastrophe. He put to work the style he had developed throughout his life and had honed as Texas governor.

People have always underestimated him. In fact, some handicappers have rated him the fourth best politician in his family (after his father, mother, and brother Jeb). None have ever given him good odds for success. Yet time after time, he has exceeded expectations. He has proven himself a surprisingly effective executive—a "reformer with results," as he promised during his 2000 presidential campaign. His easygoing outward manner masks a tough, decisive executive who has consistently performed far better as a political leader than almost anyone had imagined.

Just as important, he has lured opponents and skeptics into underestimating him. Some of that comes from the image of the amiable dunce he has never been able to shake. Some of it comes from the fact that his core skills aren't analytical. Rather, they come from his finely tuned skill of building a team and then using that team to make decisions.

Bush has a style that works for him and that fits his approach to management. As Vance McMahan, former policy director for Bush in Austin, remarked, "It's often said he's a man comfortable in his own skin—and I think that's exactly right."

Bush has a core set of ideas about what makes a good manager. He knows himself, he knows what works for him, and he uses that style to guide his decisions with laserlike precision.

Lawrence B. Lindsey, who had served in both the Reagan and first Bush administrations before becoming a governor of the Federal Reserve Board and a Bush economic adviser, told a reporter during the 2000 campaign, "The thing that struck me most about Bush early on was how thoroughly comfortable with himself he was."

Lindsey had brought together economists to advise the campaign. He found, "He's really a CEO. He asks us for our advice and we give it. Of course, if you have six economists, you get seven opinions. Then he calls the shots."

Lindsey also discovered that Bush wasn't shy about reject-
ing advice he didn't find helpful. "He's very much a Texan,"
he explained, "and I was once on the receiving end of a very
straight-shooting response that one would not want to see
printed."

Historians will undoubtedly take generations to decide
on his legacy. Policy wonks will battle over whether he's
made right or wrong decisions. Friends will praise him for
his leadership, and foes will criticize him for his mistakes.
However, it's impossible to escape the central fact: Bush has
a distinctive management style that shapes his decisions
and, indeed, his presidency. It's as clear and powerful a style
as any president has brought to the Oval Office. Thus, to
understand Bush, it's essential first to understand his style.
And even to begin charting his legacy will require starting
first with the way he approaches the job.

Bill Clinton used to complain quietly that he was des-
tined never to be a great president because history never
dealt him great problems. From his first days, Bush certainly never had that worry—history dealt him great problems,
in spades. Bill Clinton also used to talk about building a
bridge to the 21st century. He argued that the Reagan-Bush
years marked not only the end of the 20th century, but also
the end of a generation of public policy. Clinton hoped to
define the new policies that would shape America for the
next generation, but the failure of his health-care plan, his
battle with Newt Gingrich and the congressional
Republicans, his extramarital affair, and his impeachment
by Congress made that impossible.

History, in fact, might conclude that Clinton was a bridge
to the 21st century—but that the presidency of George W.
Bush was on the other side. Whether that is history's judg-

ment—or whether Bush, like Clinton, ends up as another transitional figure en route to yet another new reality—depends on how Bush uses his style to shape the nation's policy.

What's the core of the Bush style? Is it his training as an MBA? After all, Bush is the nation's first MBA president, a 1975 graduate of the Harvard Business School. For years, private sector managers have contended that government would work much better if it operated according to business practice. Once in government, many of them found out the hard way that many business strategies didn't work in the public sector and that government presented its own unique and daunting challenges. Is Bush living proof that strategic, disciplined, team-based MBA strategy can work in government?

Or is it Bush's leadership? Bush has approached a wide range of jobs, from co-ownership of the Texas Rangers baseball team to the Texas governorship, in much the same way as he has subsequently managed the presidency. After middling success, at best, as a business executive, he hit his stride in elective office. Is Bush proof that leadership rests in the leader—and that understanding this particular leader requires an uncommonly subtle analysis?

George W. Bush entered the White House with a keen sense of how he would seize the reins. It was a sense centered on building and nurturing a team. He is not—indeed, he never has been—a man centered on himself. In fact, as former aide McMahan explained, "He was somebody who has as little degree of pretension as anyone I've ever met. You'd think that someone exposed to the life experiences he was would be full of himself—but that was the furthest thing from the truth."

Closer to the truth is the fact that Bush is a naturally gregarious guy who has an easy way with people and relies heavily on an executive team. The key to understanding Bush the leader lies in understanding how Bush leads and manages *his* team.

As with any style, Bush's approach to management contains tactics that help make him highly effective—and elements that can pose big problems. He builds his style on teamwork, but his insight is only as good as the vision of his team. "Groupthink" can blind leaders to problems they ought to solve but fail to see. He believes in building on past success, but the more success grows the more it can tempt leaders to overreach. He is a remarkably decisive leader, but determined leaders can weaken themselves by moving too far beyond their base of support.

Bush has a surprising record of success as a political executive. He's consistently surprised people by making effective decisions. However, it's one thing to do things well. It's another to do the right things. As president, George W. Bush has faced some of the toughest policy problems in a generation. The ultimate test of his style and the definitive judgment of his presidency will hinge on whether his style enables him to execute the right decisions—or whether it lures him down the wrong roads. The puzzle is as fascinating as for any president in American history.

What follows are the leadership ideas and methods of America's 43rd president, an individual who has tried to surround himself with the best and to bring out the best in them.

BUILDING
THE BUSH TEAM

The Making of an MBA President

"I wanted to be my own boss."

—GEORGE W. BUSH ON APPLYING TO BUSINESS SCHOOL

"George spent a lot of time learning from other people ... Those who were book-oriented would think he wasn't a serious student, but he was a serious student of people."

—ROBERT MCCALLUM,
BUSH'S FRIEND AT HARVARD BUSINESS SCHOOL

LEO CORBETT WAS SURPRISED by the apparent shift in priorities when he moved across the Charles River from Harvard College to Harvard Business School. Dinner conversations for his undergraduate class of 1970 revolved around politics and Vietnam. Many of his Harvard classmates talked politics, expecting to reach lofty political positions inside the Beltway, as Washington, D.C., was called. But when he started business school in 1973, he found that students "had become very serious and didn't want to be distracted by these outside issues."

The go-go economic boom of the 1960s had dissolved into oil shocks and high inflation. The romanticism that had once characterized what students felt for John F. Kennedy's New Frontier and Lyndon B. Johnson's War on Poverty evaporated in the face of the ongoing Vietnam War. As students worried more about their economic prospects, business and law schools seemed to offer secure futures, and competition for admission became intense. Dinner table conversations shifted away from politics and war and to the far more practical topic of how to secure good jobs.

One of Corbett's Harvard Business School classmates, George W. Bush, didn't talk politics much either—but for different reasons. Few American families had deeper political roots. His father George H. W. Bush, was chairman of the Republican National Committee at the time. His grandfather, Prescott Bush, had represented Connecticut in the U.S. Senate. But the younger Bush admitted, "I wasn't political then."

Born into a family of privilege, he had drifted through a series of jobs without finding direction. Unlike many of his classmates, Bush was searching for himself.

MAKING THE MBA MAN

George W. Bush, a middling C-average college student at Yale, had failed to be admitted to the University of Texas law school, and that failure embarrassed him. Page Keeton, the law school dean, wrote to one of those who had recommended Bush for admission, "I am sure your Mr. Bush has all the amiable qualities you describe and so will find a place at one of many fine institutions around the country. But not at the University of Texas."

Bush had to confront a very basic question: What was he going to do with his life? It was an uneasy time for the young man, and the law school rejection only underscored his problems. After graduating from two of New England's most select institutions, Phillips Academy and Yale University, Bush had served in the Texas Air National Guard, but that didn't prove to be a good career match. He worked as a management trainee for a Houston agribusiness company. He tried his hand at several political campaigns. His summer jobs included delivering mail and messages at a law firm and providing customer service at a stock brokerage. He worked on a ranch and roughnecked on an oil rig.

Still, it seemed that Bush hadn't found his niche, but he knew he liked entrepreneurial work, and a Yale friend suggested that he try business school. So he sent his application off to Harvard, without thinking much about it. "I had not yet settled on a path in life," he said and thought that business school might provide it.

Admission to Harvard Business School was tough in the early 1970s, with 3300 applicants seeking seats in the 800-student class. Bush decided to give it a try, but wanting to avoid the embarrassment if it didn't work out, he didn't tell his parents about the application. The admissions committee was impressed by his written application, and to his surprise, he was offered entrance into the class of 1975.

Bush was older than most of his business school classmates, and by now he had a wide range of business experience—most on the front lines or the shop floor. He wrote later that the experience helped educate him "to know that [business] was not what I wanted to do with my life. I had a taste of many different jobs but none of them had ever seemed to fit."

"SKY DECKER" AT CAPITALISM'S WEST POINT

The taxi driver who first dropped him off at the school told him, "Here you are at the West Point of capitalism." Bush in fact treated Harvard Business School as a serious cadet would, and that marked a big change from his college days. As an undergraduate, he took his partying seriously and quickly developed an easy rapport with his classmates.

As his close friend Roland W. Betts recalled, while other students were still adjusting to freshman life, "George was the person who in three months knew the name of everybody and actually knew 50 percent of the class."

As an undergraduate Bush had been elected president of the Yale chapter of Delta Kappa Epsilon, renowned for its parties and sports talk. In business school he pushed aside the parties and focused more on the books. As Bush recalled later, "I studied, and ran and rode my bike a lot. I was there to learn, and that's exactly what I did."

On weekends he partied at a country music club in Boston and escaped whenever he could to his parents' home in Kennebunkport, Maine. But by most accounts, he made himself into a serious student.

In one class, Bush found himself occupying the "Sky Deck," the back row of the theater-style classroom. As Charles Braxton, a former classmate, recollected, "He was the perfect Sky Decker. He wanted to take it all in, hear everybody, and pick his spot to make a big-picture comment."

Bush proved himself a student with a broad outlook, a sense for the mega-issue—and an instinct for humor and mischief. The professor in one class session explored paper flow in the office of one of the state's senators, Edward M. Kennedy. One of the students challenged the instructor to explain why that was relevant in a business course. The professor replied that someone in the class might someday become president of the United States. From his Sky Deck seat, Bush shot both arms in the air to convey the famous Nixon "V for victory" gesture.

THE "TEAMWORK" MBA

Though Bush distinguished himself for his easygoing ways, he did not set himself apart as one of the business school's top scholars. Howard Stevenson, one of his professors recalled that Bush "wrote a decent essay." Another professor, Michael E. Porter—who later became an economic policy adviser to the Bush campaign—agreed that Bush "was not a star academic performer."

He didn't excel, but his diligence did put him in the middle of the pack. However, everyone who knew him agreed that he displayed unusual charisma and teamwork. For example, when students were put to work on a three-day, schoolwide business simulation exercise. Bush's class section elected him one of the team presidents. Though his team did not win the competition, Porter told them that their collegiality would probably have produced the best results over the long haul. Bush, Porter remembered later, "was very good at getting along with people and getting things done."

The field of business was undergoing a fundamental change. In the 1960s, business expertise was by-the-numbers, focused on sharpening strategy, analyzing alternatives, and maximizing the bottom line. By the time Bush entered the Harvard Business School, this numbers-driven model was losing its appeal. His professors believed that it was no longer useful for a leader to set strategy by *knowing* the right thing to do, through expertise and in-depth analysis; that approach had led to some well-publicized failures, like the Ford Edsel. In government, it had led to Vietnam. So business schools developed a new approach, which held that no manager could know everything—that expertise was based in the knowledge an organization's employees developed, and that a smart leader built a strong team that could marshal that knowledge.

The cases students studied taught them to look and listen carefully, to learn from past mistakes, and to build a business plan for action. Students learned to be leaders by talking with—and listening to—their team members, by making tough strategic decisions, by writing a business plan for action, and then by relying on the team to carry out the plan. Most of all, the business school's case method and the Socratic question-and-answer teaching style hammered home the lesson that there is no right answer for most hard problems. Leaders had to be adept at analyzing problems carefully, understanding the issues at the core, and then coming to judgments about how best to solve them.

The team-building spirit spilled over to a culture of cultivating contacts—social, business, and political. Bush particularly thrived in that part of his education. He did better in class participation than in written exams. In one intense case-preparation session with his teammates, he dove enthusiastically into a survey of area hardware stores to discover who carried the product they were studying and how they tried to sell it. His classmates remember him as an easygoing entrepreneur, an irreverent guy who was easy to work with, a leader who led through his ability to connect with people.

Afterward, in his later career, Bush never made much of his business school background. His campaign biography, *A Charge to Keep*, spends only a few pages discussing his Harvard days, and little of that focuses on what he learned there. In his failed 1978 run for a congressional seat in West Texas, his opponent seized on the Harvard MBA to label him an elitist. Bush has long worked to reconcile his privileged upbringing with his easy personal style. It is no doubt the reason he developed an aw-shucks, plain-talking, populist streak, and downplayed the business degree.

It's clear, though, that while resisting the MBA label, Bush embraced the new MBA team-based approach. He was more a student of people than of books. He focused on the big picture rather than on the little details. He relied heavily on teamwork and worked hard to build strong bonds among his team members. In case after case—his prep school days at Phillips Academy, where he pulled together a cheerleading squad; his stint as fraternity president; his leadership of the business school study groups—Bush found himself at the center of the action by becoming the center of the team.

The team-based relationships have, in many cases, led to lifelong friendships and invaluable campaign help. Many of his Harvard Business School friends became contributors and fund-raisers. Classmate Al Hubbard, for one, put together Bush's campaign team. Just as Bush had hoped when he surprised his parents in applying, the MBA did indeed change his horizon. The central lesson of his MBA education was the role of teamwork.

ARBUSTO TO THE WHITE HOUSE

With his MBA, Bush's style blossomed. But it took some time to put it to work. After earning his degree, he returned to Midland, Texas, where his father had prospered in the oil business—and where he had lived an earlier life as a partying bachelor. He formed his own oil company and christened it "Arbusto," the Spanish word for "Bush." He achieved only moderate success as an oilman. In 1978 he launched a campaign for a seat in the U.S. House of Representatives. Bush was a hugely successful fund-raiser but a distinctly unsuccessful candidate. He lost the race by six percentage points.

If his political efforts foundered and his oil business only modestly prospered, Bush did secure one large victory. In 1977 he met and married Laura Welch, a librarian and teacher, who has since been his anchor. She was one of the few people who could look Bush in the eye and tell him he needed to shift his tone or his message. After the September 11 attacks, for example, Bush said he was going to get the terrorists, "dead or alive." The first lady worried that such harsh words would make him seem too much like a West Texas tough guy, and she told her husband more than once to soften his rhetoric. Laura Bush has long proven a balance to the more exuberant side of his personality, and she has helped provide his internal compass.

Bush's jump into big-time politics came in 1987, when he moved to Washington to help his father's successful campaign for the presidency. He had no official title, but he carried enormous weight. His father relied on him for advice, and he worked to ensure that the election team worked closely together. He moved back to Dallas after the election, but still served as a closet adviser—and occasional heavy to resolve internal staff disputes on the White House team. From his unique perch, he gathered strong insights about what did—and didn't—work in the Oval Office.

In Dallas, he shifted to a completely different line of work. Bush assembled a team of investors to resuscitate the Texas Rangers, a troubled baseball franchise since its days as the Washington Senators. He used his old-boy ties to help revive the team. In the process, he earned a huge profit, turning his initial $600,000 investment into $15 million when the owners sold the team in 1998.

His baseball ties quickly linked him to important political figures. In 1994 he parlayed these connections into a campaign for governor and surprised everyone by defeating the incumbent, Democrat Ann Richards. As governor, he relied heavily on a team of close advisers to push through a massive property tax cut and a major tort reform bill. He won reelection in 1998 by a resounding margin and became the first governor in Texas history to win back-to-back races.

His success made him a front-runner for the 2000 Republican presidential nomination. His campaign started lean, with just a small team of his most trusted advisers. Karen Hughes was his longtime press secretary. Joe Allbaugh served as Bush's chief of staff, and Karl Rove was, in Bush's own words, his "political guru." Sometimes the campaign caravan consisted of just the four of them packed into a single vehicle. Hughes later joked that, often, "the motorcade was one car and he [Bush] was sometimes driving it."

He carefully staged his entry into the campaign, pledging not to announce his candidacy until after the Texas legislative session had been completed. When he did throw his hat into the ring, he did it with a razor-sharp message from which he rarely deviated. He was a "compassionate conservative," a "reformer with results," who pledged to restore dignity to the White House and avoid the international "nation-building" forays that, he believed, had proven disastrous in the Clinton administration. Even his critics noted that he managed to hold his own in the presidential debates and in later debates mastered the details of foreign policy that seemed to stump him early on. For a candidate dueling with the intellectual Al Gore, that was no small feat.

For George W. Bush, the 2000 presidential election was the moment that focused his life and skills as nothing else ever had. His personality, his training, and his experience had all built slowly toward that point. When he was elected, the question was, how would the first MBA ever to become president of the United States apply his style to the most difficult management job in the world?

The Bush Leadership Style

"Every man who takes office in Washington either grows or swells, and when I give a man an office, I watch him carefully to see whether he is growing or swelling."

—PRESIDENT WOODROW WILSON

" … he does have a strong belief in providence, and in the necessity of gathering information, making good choices, doing your best, and trusting the result to God. That is a very strong personal belief on his part."

—BUSH SPEECHWRITER MICHAEL GERSON

WHEN GEORGE W. BUSH moved into the White House on January 20, 2001, he faced a situation no business executive has ever encountered. More than half of the people involved in choosing him had voted for someone else. Half of the people on his board of directors—the Congress—were determined to see him fail. Sly observers wrote off his chances for success before he took the oath of office, and many were looking past him to his successor. The first rule for leadership is to lead. But that's a difficult task when the deck is so badly stacked against you.

It wasn't the first time Bush had faced such long odds. He walked into the Texas governor's office with less power than almost every other governor in the nation, yet he parlayed his weak hand into presidential qualifications. When Bush championed his Texas record in the run for the White House, he even won surprising support from some of the state's legislative Democrats.

The Oval Office job, of course, is much harder. It's eaten up some governors, like Jimmy Carter, who never quite made the jump from state house to White House. Other governors have used their state politics background to fashion more successful presidencies—Ronald Reagan from the right, Bill Clinton from the left (until scandal knocked him off the tracks). The job is toughest when the problems are great and, as was the case for Bush, the leader faces virtually an antimandate for a claim to presidential power.

In the end, George W. Bush made the leap to the White House as successfully as any president in modern times, despite the odds. He capitalized on the base of power the job itself gave him. He used his style to build popular support as well as policy victories. At the core, he proved himself master of the "bully pulpit," President Theodore Roosevelt's term for the use of the White House platform to press an aggressive policy agenda. He not only borrowed part of Roosevelt's style, he also lived by one of Roosevelt's mottos: "Whenever you are asked if you can do a job, tell 'em, 'Certainly I can!' Then get busy and find out how to do it."

DON'T START WITHOUT A BUSINESS PLAN

Bush got busy running the country by crafting a business plan for the transition and his initial months in the White House even while the outcome of the election was still in doubt. During the interminable vote-counting in Florida, Gore often seemed the senior partner in the team of lawyers fighting the case. Bush, on the other hand, left the legal battle to longtime family adviser and former secretary of state James A. Baker III. Bush publicly went about the business of being governor while more quietly working on the transition to the presidency. It was a two-pronged strategy, in part to signal to the country that he fully expected to win the recount and in part to make sure he got a fast start on the job.

In less than three weeks he completed the task of naming his cabinet. He then made a ten-year tax cut his top policy priority. The projected budget surplus was huge, and he wanted to lock up the money before Congress could spend it. Some analysts though it was unwise to make the revenue evaporate before anyone knew how much new programs and a fix for social security might cost. But Bush was determined to follow the Reagan model: shrink revenue to drive down spending—don't use available revenue to fuel it.

That put the Democrats in a terrible box. They could oppose Bush's plans, look like fans of higher taxes or of big government—or both. Or they could support Bush, share the political benefits of a tax cut, and give the president a quick victory. By a surprisingly large and quick margin, he won his tax cut.

Following the tax vote, Bush focused on his education agenda. As governor, he had championed better schools. In the campaign, he argued that local schools ought to meet tough standards or lose their federal aid. He was promoting this phase of his strategy, in fact, when he visited a Florida classroom on the morning of September 11.

Finally, Bush envisioned a foreign policy initiative, especially to deal with Iraq and his belief that Iraq had weapons of mass destruction. He and his advisers saw Saddam Hussein as a substantial threat, and he wanted to deal with Hussein before the Iraqi leader had a chance to cause mischief.

In the meantime, of course, the September 11 terrorist attacks intervened. Bush had no choice but to push his education and domestic policy agenda to the back burner and focus on foreign policy. In addition, his attention overseas was focused, out of necessity, on al Qaeda and Osama bin Laden, not Saddam Hussein. Bush and his advisers quickly had to retool their business plan to make security within the United States their first job. It was to their advantage that they already had experience at retooling, experience that had already led to Bush's big tax cut success.

MAKE THE BUREAUCRACY FIT YOUR PERSONALITY

Beyond the business plan was a set of basic rules to guide how the White House staff worked and behaved. "This is the only bureaucracy in Washington that can change to fit the personality of the president," chief of staff Andrew H. Card, Jr. told a reporter. "This president is the first ever to have an MBA." Bush was determined to impress his style on the White House—and to push out the influences of the Clinton team.

Close observers were astounded at the difference from the Clinton years. In putting together his first budget, Card estimated that Bush invested about five hours in meetings. In contrast, in his initial weeks, Bill Clinton spent 25 hours in formal meetings and twice that amount in casual conversations. Bush quickly worked his way through the basic options and made his strategic decisions. He preferred oral briefings, short background memos, and quick decisions. Clinton wanted to know all the details, to talk about them with a wide circle of advisers, and to explore the implications before deciding.

In fact, Bush and Clinton shared some points of style. Both are strong "people persons." Clinton was at his best in public settings where he could reach out and touch those attending. Countless members of his audiences talked about how they connected with him, even in very large gatherings. He struck a strong and powerful note on television. Bush hasn't shown the same magnetism in large crowds. His early television appearances were strained, though he improved with experience. But even his toughest critics point to his warm personal style in meetings. He likes people and connects easily and informally with them.

There's no better sign of that connection than Bush's famous habit of bestowing nicknames on friends and staffers. Virtually anyone he encounters is fair game. The president might say, "Get me Knuckles on the line," or "Where's the Eskimo?" or "Let Bones and Uptown handle this." The problem is, sometimes nobody has a clue as to who he's talking about.

Along the way, Bush has collected his own nicknames: "Georgie," "Little George," "Bushtail," "Tweeds," "Lip," "Temporary," "Bombastic Bushkin," and of course, "Dubya" (the Texas version of his middle initial, W). Sources report that First Lady Laura calls him "Bushie."

ESTABLISH RULES EARLY AND STICK TO THEM

If the nicknames mark Bush's informal side, he has a tough, formal, disciplined side as well. Soon after taking office, he imposed a set of White House rules. The contrast with the Clinton years could not have been more stark. Chief of Staff Card laid them out:

- **Attire: suit and tie required.** Gone was the informal Clinton dress code. Aides often wore blue jeans and T-shirts to meetings, even in the Oval Office. Bush insisted that men wear jackets and ties at all times in the Oval Office. Women were required to wear business attire. Card reported he hadn't seen the president in the Oval Office without a suit and tie. Clinton, by contrast, was often observed wandering around the White House in his jogging clothes (sweats and sneakers).

- **Brevity is a must.** Bush limited briefing papers to a page—two at most. Clinton read voraciously. Bush insisted that aides boil issues down to their core. "He doesn't like memos that state the obvious," Card explained.

- **Be punctual.** Bush is ruthless in starting—and stopping—meetings. "The president begins meetings on time and ends them on time," Card said curtly. During the 7:00 A.M. senior staff meetings, he has stopped aides in mid-sentence at precisely 7:58 A.M. so he can join the president's 8:00 A.M. intelligence briefing. The previous administration, by contrast, ran by what aides and reporters jokingly referred to as "Clinton standard time." Clinton would allow freewheeling meetings to linger long past their allotted time, and public events might not begin until hours after their scheduled start.

- **Treat everyone with respect.** Card reminded everyone "that we are just staffers, and no more important than anyone working at HHS or HUD or the Department of Transportation—or the people opening the mail." Bush told staffers he expected them to return each other's phone calls promptly, a sharp contrast with the Clinton years, when unanswered phone messages often littered people's desks.

- **Develop healthy work habits.** Bush sharply told his staffers not to be workaholics. The president customarily leaves the office by 6:30 P.M. He expects staffers to spend time with their families, and he rarely interrupts their personal time with evening phone calls. Bush has kept to his routine. Bill Clinton, in contrast, was a night-person president. He often launched a second workday after dinner, spending hours on the phone, late into the night, talking with aides and advisers.

DEVELOP YOUR OWN LEADERSHIP STYLE

Bush is the very model of a modern MBA president. He builds his approach to the presidency on teamwork, especially in his West Wing staff. He builds a clear strategy and a business plan for implementing it. Unlike Bill Clinton, he has remained focused on a small agenda. He keeps his message sharp and focused. At a visit to the Pentagon less than a week after September 11, he told reporters, "I want justice," and that meant tracking down Osama bin Laden. "And there's a poster out West, as I recall, that said, 'Wanted: Dead or Alive.'"

Few presidents have been that blunt. Bush insists on tough discipline among his staffers, with a tightly controlled flow of information in and out. Press secretary Ari Fleischer even refused to disclose what the First Family ate at their first presidential Thanksgiving dinner (although word later leaked out that they dined on turkey, green beans, sweet potato puree, and pumpkin pie). The contrast with Bill Clinton, whose staff was prone to leak information, could scarcely have been sharper.

Of course, all presidents—indeed, all leaders—develop their own distinctive styles. Clinton relished the details, while Bush celebrates the MBWA (management by walking around) approach. Some, like Clinton, like to dive into paper and aren't happy without their hands in details, while others, like Bush, focus on the big decisions and delegate to subordinates the job of carrying them out. Some are morning people, while others are night owls. But unlike all managers, style is more significant in the White House, for reasons we'll go into below.

AN UNUSUAL JOB

The scope of the job a president confronts is far larger than anything in the private sector. The risk of failure is great and the consequences enormous. Presidents have tight limits on deciding which markets to enter or which products to develop. If a war in Bosnia or a battle against inflation goes badly, the president can't simply decide to abandon a product line. Presidents can't easily reorganize their operations to increase efficiency or focus on a new strategy.

Bush's protracted struggle with Congress over the Department of Homeland Security, which was eventually approved, showed how hard it can be to shuffle the organizational boxes. In the private sector, boards of directors support corporate leaders—or they fire them. In government, Congress is the president's board of directors, and Congress has a vested interest in many of the existing work patterns. And just as the president can't fire them, members of Congress can't fire him (only impeach him, and the odds of that are slim). At any given time, half of them might be working against him, trying to make him fail politically.

In other words, presidents can't simply give orders to make things work. In 1952, Harry S. Truman suggested what would happen if the voters elected Dwight Eisenhower president. "He'll sit here," Truman said, "and he'll say, 'Do this! Do that!' *And nothing will happen.* Poor Ike—it won't be a bit like the Army. He'll find it very frustrating." Indeed, Truman quipped, "All the president is, is a glorified public relations man who spends his time flattering, kissing, and kicking people to get them to do what they are supposed to do anyway." Truman, as it turned out, underestimated Eisenhower, just as many observers underestimated Bush. Author Fred Greenstein found that Eisenhower proved remarkably effective as an executive, with a "hidden hand" style that wasn't obvious on the surface but which, behind the scenes, galvanized his staff behind effective policy.

That is why style is so important to the president. In the absence of many of the resources private managers depend upon, presidents must cajole, threaten, stroke, bellow, coo, smile, and scowl. Most of all, they must persuade, as Richard E. Neustadt concluded in his celebrated book, *Presidential Power*. Their ability to persuade depends on their style—so it's essential that the style fits them and the job they have to do.

Franklin Roosevelt soothed a worried nation as a fatherly figure who delivered fireside chats. Truman was sharp, blunt, but funny. Eisenhower imposed a style as much corporate as military on the White House. Kennedy brought youthful vigor, new intellectual curiosity, and hard-headed McNamara-style analysis. Johnson was famous for "the treatment." He could be bellicose and warm, threatening and reassuring, charming and gruff, all within the same conversation. He would mix the approaches, keeping people on edge as he searched for the right weapon to get his way. Johnson staffers often told tales of reluctant members of Congress who set out with Johnson on a one-on-one stroll around the White House grounds, only to return as the president's supporters.

Nixon's boldness opened the door to China, but his paranoia undermined his presidency. Ford sought to be a healing figure. Carter tried to bring a common touch by

walking down Pennsylvania Avenue following his inauguration and sporting a cardigan sweater in his own fireside
chat. Reagan proved a populist "great communicator" on
television, while Bush (number 41) was more patrician.
Clinton felt voters' pain.

The president's style matters because, more than anything else, it determines whether he can be the master of
events—or whether they will master him. The style is the
prism through which presidents sort through competing
ideas to frame their agenda. It is the tool they use to pursue
the agenda, both in the political arena and with the public.
It is the template that presidents employ in sorting through
the new, unpredictable crises that predictably pop up in
every administration. It is the pattern that shapes work with
the president's staff and in the end determines how the president weathers the oppressive stress of the presidency itself.

BUSH'S STYLE

George W. Bush unquestionably has a clear style. Unlike
Kennedy's, it is not built on blazing intellect, and unlike
Johnson's, it is not built on unrelenting personal pressure. It
shares some of the same amiable qualities of Reagan's
approach to government, but it also has surprising elements
of the shrewd style that Eisenhower brought to the White
House. Unpacking his presidency to discover that style
takes some doing, because what we see on television often
does not match the way Bush works in the Oval Office. It
requires understanding his family, his political roots, and
the subtle way they shape his approach to the job.

As much as anything, though, Bush is the prototype of
the MBA executive who took over the biggest organization

in the world. The question is whether the organization is a good fit for his MBA skills. Henry Mintzberg and Joseph Lampel, two management experts who have studied why CEOs fail, warn that they tend to do so in similar ways: "They ran their businesses according to a formula, regardless of the people involved or the dynamics of the industry in question." In fact, they warn, there's a connection with the MBA degree. "The MBA tends to be heavy on the 'B' and light on the 'A,' teaching business functions, yet not developing the practice of administering." MBAs are strong on making decisions and framing policy. They sometimes tend to be weak on "the messy reality in which decisions are executed."

Does Bush have what it takes not only to frame strategy but to produce results? If he is a true MBA manager, is he light on the "A"—the administration—side? That can be a drawback of MBA training, Mintzberg and Lampel warn, because the programs teach through the case method: "Students with little or no management experience are presented with 20 pages on a company they do not know and told to pronounce on its strategy the next day."

What about a president, especially one without substantial experience in many domestic policy problems and little experience in most international ones, who works off one-page briefing memos, reaches sharp judgments, and frames them in terms like "Wanted: Dead or Alive"?

In part, the answers to these tough questions grow from his roots. He is the first son of an American president to be elected in 175 years. He also brings political experience from a successful Texas governorship. Together they combine to frame a distinctive style that has framed his presidency.

BUSH LESSONS

- **Don't start without a plan.** Bush began crafting his plan before the vote count in Florida was finished. This helped him to hit the ground running when the dust settled. The lesson is clear: Establish a plan, and implement it early. That might mean the difference between success and failure.

- **Make the organization fit your personality.** Bush imposed his ways on the Oval Office, not the other way around. He starts and ends meetings on time, insists on a suit and tie, yet simultaneously imposes a certain degree of informality with staffers and journalists. That's his way, and he uses it to his advantage.

- **Keep focused on the task at hand.** Bush watches the small things to sharpen his focus on the key tasks at hand. After September 11, 2001, Bush focused virtually his entire presidency on fighting terrorism. He understood that his administration had a new charter, and made sure that his inner circle brought the same degree of focus.

- **Develop your own leadership style.** One of the key lessons that can be learned from Bush's first years in office is that leaders must develop their own style. All presidents and leaders have their own idiosyncrasies and preferences. Do not simply assume the role of your predecessor. It may sound obvious, but it's a point that's often missed: Being true to your own style may mean the difference between success and failure.

The Teamwork Imperative

"I'm not afraid to surround myself with strong and competent people."

—GEORGE W. BUSH, ON NAMING HIS CABINET

"Individual commitment to a team effort—that is what makes a team work, a company work, a society work, a civilization work."

—VINCE LOMBARDI

EVEN MORE THAN MOST EXECUTIVES, the American president must rely on a strong team. The problems are huge, and the costs of a misstep can be staggering. Choosing the best policy options requires a keen sense of the core problems and the most solid information available. Getting that information, however, is tough. The president is constantly surrounded by the Secret Service, monitored by television film crews, and trailed by reporters.

That makes it hard for the president to get a good pulse on what people are thinking, to gauge what is happening beyond the White House gates, and to understand the most important issues of the day. The president lies at the bottom of an enormous funnel that distills vast quantities of information—from figures on retail sales to assessment of guerrilla movements in the Philippines—into short, digestible memos.

What he knows he learns from a vast store of information boiled down by his staff. He constantly risks being overwhelmed by unimportant detail and blinded to critical facts. That is true for all executives, of course, but even more so for the president. The fundamental difference is that the stakes for presidential decision-making are incalculably higher than anything in the private sector.

Bush came to the White House as the only president to have worked there before taking office. Perhaps no president in history started the job better schooled in the intricacies of the Oval Office. He had served his father as a closet adviser on policy and process. On occasion he even served as hatchet man, to fire high-level staff members—like onetime chief of staff John Sununu—that no one else could touch. It was during the first years of his father's presidency that Sununu tightly controlled access to the Oval Office. Advisers who wanted to talk to the president first had to be cleared by Sununu. This created enormous frustration among aides, who jockeyed for position and on occasion leaked stories to the media to get their message to the president. It also caused serious problems for the president, who sometimes found himself shielded from advice and the bad news he needed to hear. Number 41 trusted his son more than any of his advisers, and when a consensus emerged that Sununu had to go, W delivered the news.

The lesson of surrounding himself with a solid, trustworthy team was not lost on Bush 43. He came away from his White House experiences with a sense of what had worked well for his father and what had served his father poorly, and later, of how he might organize his own team.

GET UNFILTERED INFORMATION

Bush wanted to avoid his father's mistakes. First as governor, and then as president, he decided to avoid the hierarchical chief-of-staff model. Instead, he created a system that gave key aides easy access, without having to go through an all-powerful chief of staff. His Texas policy adviser, Vance McMahan, recalled Bush saying:

*I want a flat structure where my key senior
staff members report directly to me. I don't want opinions
filtered through one individual.*

The chief of staff was in charge of process—making sure that what had to get done in fact got done on time. But the staff chief was not a "first among equals." For Bush 43, the most important link would be his relationship with each adviser, not their connections with each other or to a central gatekeeper.

It was this approach in Texas that "gave the senior staff members a great deal of access to the governor," McMahan further explained. "It also gave them a chance to build relationships. The information didn't get filtered."

This model also put a huge burden on the man at the top. He had to ruthlessly manage his time to avoid being swamped by the competing demands of staffers. He had to balance the competing perspectives he received. He had to make all the key decisions himself and couldn't off-load key decisions to others. He had to focus on key strategies and maintain balance in his own thinking so that decisions didn't simply reflect the views of the last aide he consulted. (This was a charge often leveled at Bill Clinton.)

Believing that this approach had worked well for him in Austin, Bush brought it with him to Washington. He created a team with the chief of staff as manager of process. Key staff members could see him without an appointment—and without having to go through anyone else. Bush was determined to make himself the center of the action, and to force his aides to deal directly with him instead of battling with each other. For a president whose style was so intimate, who so greatly valued his personal ties with his aides, it was a structure that fit.

Other presidents, notably Jimmy Carter, had tried similar approaches. Carter likewise valued personal relationships, and he was determined not to have anyone serve as Oval Office gatekeeper. For Carter, however, the structure quickly broke down. Staff members squabbled, often publicly, about their policy differences, and they elbowed for access. Carter found himself drawn into detailed decisions that had no business being on his desk, including, most famously, schedules for the White House tennis court. For Carter, a nuclear engineer with a keen eye to the most intricate details, the spokes-of-the-wheel structure proved a very poor match. It didn't take long for the model to dissolve into a more traditional hierarchical chief-of-staff model, with Hamilton Jordan in the key position.

According to White House personnel chief Clay Johnson, Bush "did not want someone to be chief of staff who was overterritorial, or was a control freak, or felt like they had to control the content or the recommendations that flowed to the president." Instead, his emphasis was on a staff chief "who was more a facilitator, an orchestrator, and a tie breaker."

The conventional wisdom among analysts is that the hub-and-spoke model is deceptively attractive to new presidents. It offers the promise of congeniality, but it sows the seeds of internal civil war. Most presidencies drift to a strong chief of staff, if for no other reason than to manage the unceasing flow of paper and people into the Oval Office. Bush resisted that drift. His structure encountered fewer bumps in the road, both during the transition and in his first years in office, than any recent president.

The reason is Bush himself. He has served as his own chief of staff on matters of substance because of his notable self-discipline—and because he hires strong and effective managers to work for him. Journalists tripped over themselves in calling his foreign policy advisers a national security "dream team." With the exception of his first team of economic advisers, who were compelled to resign after the midterm elections, analysts called his cabinet one of the strongest on record. When asked by reporters to describe what his personnel choices said about his management style, Bush replied:

I hope the American people realize that a good executive is one that understands how to recruit people and how to delegate, how to align authority and responsibility, how to hold people accountable for results, and how to build a team of people.

BUILDING TEAM BUSH

Bush decided to run his Oval Office so that his five closest White House aides could see him at any point, without having to go through anyone first. The five insider players were:

- **Andrew H. Card, Jr., chief of staff.** Card served Bush 41 as secretary of transportation and, before that, as deputy chief of staff. He was President Reagan's liaison to the nation's governors and mayors. During the Clinton years, he headed the American Automobile Manufacturers Association, the trade association for the nation's car makers. As chief of staff, he has served as Bush 43's process manager, to make sure that things needing to get done are done. But he was not the gatekeeper to the Oval Office.

- **Condoleezza Rice, national security adviser.** She former-
  ly was provost—the chief operating officer—at Stanford
  University. During the first Bush administration, she
  worked on the National Security Council as the president's adviser on Soviet and East European affairs. Rice
  joined the Bush campaign early in the race and visited
  Austin often to tutor the candidate on foreign policy. It
  was little surprise, therefore, that she moved to
  Washington to head the NSC. She has carefully worked
  to balance the foreign policy advice the president
  receives. She usually holds her counsel until after everyone has left and the president is weighing his decisions.

- **Ari Fleischer, press secretary.** Before joining the Bush
  presidential campaign in the fall of 1999, Fleischer was
  communications director for Elizabeth Dole's unsuccessful White House run. He worked on Capitol Hill as press
  secretary for Senator Pete Domenici (R., N.M.) and then
  as spokesman for the U.S. House of Representatives
  Ways and Means Committee. He proved tough in dealing
  with reporters in the always rough-and-tumble daily
  press briefings, and worked constantly to make sure his
  words framed the message.

- **Karen Hughes, counselor to the president.** Hughes has
  had one of the longest and closest relationships with
  Bush. She was a former television reporter and executive
  director of the Texas Republican Party, and a member of
  the Bush team since he took the governorship. Insiders
  ranked her with Karl Rove as the president's closest
  advisers, and they say she knows Bush so well she can
  finish his sentences for him. When she left the White
  House to move her family back to Austin, analysts won-

dered how her departure would affect the team. She remained in close telephone contact with Bush and visited Washington often to share her advice.

- **Karl Rove, senior White House adviser.** Close observers have called Rove "Bush's brain," for his uncanny political instincts and his ability to shape Bush's strategy. As head of his own Austin-based public affairs company, Rove masterminded Bush's gubernatorial runs. Texas law required an arm's-length relationship between the public office and political teams, so Rove did not work in the Bush governor's office. In the White House, however, there is a "permanent campaign," as political scientist Charles O. Jones has put it, and Rove has been Bush's guru for that campaign.

A sixth key adviser completes Bush's inner circle:

- **Richard B. Cheney, vice president.** Cheney is a seasoned Washington hand, having served as chief of staff in the Ford administration, a member of the House of Representatives, and secretary of defense during the first Bush administration. Cheney had sometimes scrapped with Donald Rumsfeld, secretary of defense for Bush 43, but his experience allowed him to go toe-to-toe with the capital's most powerful insiders. Bush has relied heavily on him for his political and policy judgment.

A close look at Team Bush reveals several important facts. All were strong and experienced players before he chose them. As presidential expert Charles O. Jones warns, "Working in the White House should not be your first job." The team members earned their chops in tough political combat. And while only some of them had worked with each other before, Bush had developed close working relationships with each of them. As Karl Rove explained, "Bush has tended to surround himself with people he's taken the measure of."

The process worked so seamlessly for Team Bush that it's hard to imagine an alternative. But the Clinton team operated quite differently. Clinton chose his team members more to represent important constituencies than because of their relationship with him. Hired because of what they knew and who they represented, they were harder to corral and focus. Leaks proliferated and staff-level tugs-of-war were common. Bush managed to avoid most of those snags.

Unlike some presidents who came into office with trusted advisers with little experience, or experienced advisers without a personal relationship with the president, Team Bush started with a truly unusual combination of trust and expertise. Some presidents spend the first months trying to get their team to mesh. Bush's reliance on team members he already knew and trusted, coupled with his spokes-of-the-wheel strategy, gave Team Bush a running start and ensured few snags. Few White House teams in memory got such a fast launch or worked with so few bumps.

NURTURE TALENT AND GET THE BEST FROM THEM

Team Bush would not have worked, however, without Bush's knack for nurturing his personal links with his team members. As mentioned previously, there's no better sign of that knack than his habit of bestowing nicknames on friends, staffers, government leaders, and journalists. Virtually anyone could be a fair target. One high-ranking Bush aide, known as "French" for reasons he can't fathom, joked that "internal communications are in turmoil," because aides sometimes can't figure out the nicknames.

Bush has christened Vice President Dick Cheney "Big Time." National Security Adviser Condoleezza Rice is "Guru." Defense Secretary Donald Rumsfeld is "Rummy." Communications Adviser Karen Hughes was "High Prophet," while political strategist Karl Rove is "Boy Genius." The nicknaming started inside the Bush family, where George W. Bush is "W" and his father is "41" (for the forty-first president—which makes W's alternate nickname "Number 43"). His mother, tellingly, is "Number One." Bush refers to his wife, Laura, as "First" (short for "First Lady"). Along the way, as mentioned earlier, Bush has collected his own nicknames: "Georgie," "Little George," "Bushtail," "Tweeds," "Lip," "Temporary," "Bombastic Bushkin," "Bushie," and of course "Dubya."

The informal nicknames can hide a sharp edge to Bush. Aides report that his face signals when he's engaged (with a smile and a laugh) and when he's not happy (with a piercing, unmistakable look of displeasure). If Bush is comfortable in his own skin, as everyone who knows him agrees, some of that is because he's made the White House itself part of his skin as well. He's tailored the inner working of the position to fit his style, not the other way around.

As a reporter who knew him well from Texas explained, "Bush speaks louder in body language than any politician I have ever seen." Slouching in a chair means confidence. He emphasizes his message by bobbing his head when he talks. His eyes light up when preparing a joke. His eyes and brows narrow when he is unhappy. Aides know his chuckle, "Heh," as a sign of irony. Quite simply, "He is formidable in these informal settings."

He insists on short memos. Aides quickly find that greatly raises the stakes. It's hard to boil complicated problems down to short summaries. When they begin their presentation to Bush, they often find Bush boring into the central issues and raising global questions far beyond the scope of the options memo. More than one aide has described the process as intimidating. Bush is often impatient—not because he's bored, but because he wants to identify and focus on what he considers the fundamental questions.

Bush recognizes his own impulsiveness. One way he insulates himself from the risks of rapid-fire decision-making, he told Bob Woodward, "is to make sure you listen" to experienced advisers. Such aides, he believed, were an important counterforce to his own spontaneity. He's said:

> *"If I have any genius or smarts, it's the ability
> to recognize talent, ask them to serve,
> and work with them as a team."*

He expects his aides to cut to the heart of the issue, to focus on answers instead of complex questions, to get to solutions, to catch and correct possible flaws in a plan. Bush himself plays provocateur in such debates: "One of my jobs is to be provocative, to force decisions, and to make sure in everybody's mind where we're headed."

There long have been questions about Bush's intelligence. Frank Bruni, a *New York Times* reporter who followed him for months on the campaign trail, said, "It was never clear how much he really knew and, perhaps more to the point, how diligently he was trying to amass the knowledge he might need." As Bruni put it, "This was always the rub with Bush, the great big question mark at the heart of the man." Indeed, Bush's aides have carefully managed the events at which he publicly appeared. He tended to avoid prime-time news conferences and unscripted media events. In describing one executive order, Bruni found him "so vague and off-kilter it was almost wiggy."

Bush himself makes no pretense about his intelligence. He has never presented himself as a master of facts and detail. Indeed, his opponent used his Yale and Harvard degrees against him in his first political race, and he's been careful since about pointing to his academic training. It's never quite clear whether he has little intellectual curiosity about the details—or whether he simply doesn't believe that the details are as important as the overall strategy. His MBA training—along with his fundamental instincts—have taught him that strategic, big-picture decisions matter most for top managers.

The manner in which a president digests information doesn't necessarily determine success. Details have devoured some presidents (like Carter), and detailed knowledge of the facts haven't always focused presidents on the key strategic choices they faced (like Clinton). What does matter is whether the president makes the right decisions. That is the central task of the manager and of his team.

This frames the central puzzle of Team Bush: Just how does the team work?

In practice, the team operates on a platform supported by four legs: a sharp strategy, a clearly defined message, discipline in carrying it out, and effective leverage of the assets at hand. Understanding how those four legs support the Bush platform provides the key clues for how Team Bush works—and what lessons they teach.

BUSH LESSONS

- **Create the right structure.** Bush arrived at the Oval Office knowing that he would not put a gatekeeper between him and his closest advisers. Instead, he employed a flat model built on personal relationships, to make sure that his inner circle had access to him and that he had access to them.

- **Make sure to get unfiltered information.** Top managers need all sorts of information, good and bad ... especially bad. This is why it is crucial to have a mechanism in place that ensures a steady stream of information from all quarters.

- **Hire people smarter than you are.** Bush was not afraid to hire leaders and cabinet members that people perceived were smarter than he was. The first MBA president knew that the key to success had to do with his team and his ability to exact the best performance from each of them.

- **Master the four keys of Team Bush.** Team Bush has a four-prong approach, one that takes into account a finely etched strategy, a clearly defined message, discipline in execution, and an apparatus to leverage the assets at hand.

LEADING
THE BUSH WAY

Bush as Strategist

"They can say what they want about me, but at least
I know who I am and who my friends are."

—GEORGE W. BUSH, SPEAKING TO
NBC'S ALEXANDRA PELOSI, 2002

" ... people should do what they say they are going do to, particularly in politics. ... I think that is probably the single most important tenet of his philosophy."

—TEXAS REP. PAUL SADLER,
ABOUT BUSH'S APPROACH TO POLICY AS GOVERNOR

AMERICANS HAVE LONG PRIDED themselves on setting the standards by which the world's elections ought to be run. They were certainly unprepared for the aftermath of the 2000 presidential election, with a weekslong court battle that never seemed to end. Each press conference by the warring Gore and Bush featured an escalation of American flags in the backdrop, with each side struggling to appear more presidential. The two campaigns battled over the keys to Washington's official presidential campaign headquarters—and the $5 million pot of transition funds. The nation got a painful, extended lesson in the Electoral College, perhaps the most arthritic section of America's living constitution.

Throughout it all, Team Bush had a clear and straightforward strategy. By acting as winners, they strengthened their case that they *were* the winners. They pointed to Gore's initial phone call to concede the election and quietly suggested Gore was working behind the scenes to undermine Florida law. But throughout it all, Bush stayed above the fray, focusing on key issues and assembling his cabinet. It was simple: Playing the part would make the reality.

PREPARE EARLY: THE FIRST STEPS ARE CRUCIAL

The electoral turmoil not only provided endless weeks of political theater. It also robbed Bush of the most important asset a new president has: a honeymoon with Congress, the press, and the American people. From the November 7 election, it took the courts 36 days to sort out the issues, and Gore conceded on day 37. If they concur on anything, presidential scholars agree that the first weeks of the transition are crucial to shaping a new presidency. If anything is clear about Bush's transition, however, it's that he had the right strategy to help him negotiate one of the most contentious election battles in American history.

Any new job or management assignment is tough, and putting together a presidency is one of the toughest. The president-elect needs to assemble a staff, choose a cabinet, frame the big issues, rough out a legislative agenda, and prepare a budget. Thousands of résumés, from campaign workers and ordinary citizens, fall like a blizzard on staffers trying to find desks and computers. The days from early November until the inauguration on January 20 spin by with breathtaking speed, and the new president usually needs every second to be ready to govern. Jimmy Carter's pollster, Patrick H. Caddell, said, "Most White Houses are lucky if they get the furniture in." For Bush, five weeks evaporated in the protracted election battle. That cut his preparation time in half.

Tough transitions are legendary in Washington politics. It's long been a tradition for the outgoing and incoming presidents to ride together to the Capitol for the inauguration ceremony, but relations between Dwight Eisenhower and Harry S. Truman were so frosty that Eisenhower refused even to get out of his car to greet Truman. The transition from Jimmy Carter to Ronald Reagan was downright painful. Among other things, Nancy Reagan reportedly suggested that the Carters ought to move out a few weeks early so she could redecorate the White House before inauguration day.

It's a tough job—even tougher in half the time. It's tougher yet when pundits conclude that the battle over the presidency is likely to render the new president powerless, no matter what he does. Jim Cannon was a domestic policy adviser to President Gerald Ford, another president who came into office under a cloud. "No one in the public knew much who Ford was," he told *Washington Post* columnist David Broder, but they were glad to get rid of Richard Nixon and welcomed Ford as an honest man. Ford had never been elected either vice president or president— Nixon appointed him vice president after Spiro Agnew had resigned—"but nobody ever questioned his legitimacy," Cannon said. For Bush, however, "There will always be questions about the legitimacy of [his] victory."

TEAM BUSH'S RULES FOR WINNING

To make matters worse, Bush had only a narrow Republican majority in the House of Representatives. The Senate was divided 50-50, with Vice President Cheney, presiding officer in the Senate, permitted to break ties. A pall hung over Bush's claim to power, and he couldn't count on much help from Republicans on Capitol Hill. Cannon wondered whether, with "half the voters thinking the president does not belong there, [if] anything can be done." At most, Rep. Mark E. Souder (R., Ind.) suggested, it was likely to be "a presidency of small advances rather than broad, sweeping changes." Democrats set to work to undermine the Bush agenda by reminding analysts about his weak claim to power. Only strong and quick steps toward conciliation—especially moderation in his game plan—would help him succeed, they proclaimed.

But Team Bush rejected that counsel. Chief of Staff Card prepared background memos on every transition since 1960, drawing lessons, small and large, to guide the Bush transition. To demonstrate that they were organized and in command, Card insisted that aides return phone calls quickly. To build important relationships, he wrote thank-you notes to the people he met with, and members of Congress were flattered that he took time to make the personal connection.

Bush was determined to avoid the civil wars that marked some transitions. Jimmy Carter, for example, found his campaign and transition staffs in open conflict. Those battles disrupted his transition, and his White House staff never fully recovered. In the first week after taking office, Bill Clinton drove his approval ratings into the basement by announcing support for gay people joining the military. The issue had not been fully staffed out, and he walked into a buzz saw. His problems worsened as several appointees, including his attorney general nominee, ran into trouble.

On the other end of the spectrum, Bush learned from the relatively smooth Reagan transition, in which the president kept staff struggles under control and far from the public eye. The first steps a new president takes create images, both with Washington insiders and with the people, about how firm his grip is on the levers of power. Missteps create lasting problems from which recovery is slow, painful, and almost always incomplete.

With so little time to organize and such a great chance for initial missteps to bog down a new president, it's crucial "to strike the right starting note." as Bush adviser Karl Rove noted. "Time is precious," he added. So Team Bush developed a straightforward strategy to change the perception of an illegitimate presidency and start his administration out on the right note:

- **Acting like a winner helps make you a winner.** Weeks before the election was finally settled, Bush made a victory speech but then faded from public view. His advisers told reporters that he was busy working on the transition, especially his cabinet appointments. He appeared periodically at his ranch for photo opportunities, including a notable visit by retired general Colin Powell. Andrew Card told reporters that the two discussed foreign policy issues, but the clear implication was that Powell was being considered for a key post in the new administration. Bush also met early in December with Republican congressional leaders to discuss how best to advance his legislative agenda.

  Meanwhile, Karen Hughes constantly reprocessed the same basic message: Bush won the election. Gore can't accept the outcome. The Bush team was briskly moving forward in preparing for the inevitable. Some Democrats, correctly, suggested Gore's odds of winning the court battles were low. Their comments quickly found their way into Bush press releases. Team Bush did everything they could to suggest that the extended court battle was a mere formality that in the end would confirm their victory.

- **Build a team you can trust, and don't be afraid to delegate.** Early in the process, Bush delegated to Dick Cheney the job of sorting through candidates for cabinet positions. Cheney and his team interviewed leading candidates and made recommendations to Bush. By the time the Florida outcome was decided, Bush was nearly ready to announce his team. He started by making clear who was in charge of the process, and, by naming Cheney, made it impossible for disappointed candidates or warring staffers to try end runs. That ensured greater control over the process and created a workmanlike sense of direction in the transition.

- **Know what you want—and don't cave in too soon.** Bush was under no illusion about the tenuousness of his position. If any one of several different court decisions had gone differently, Al Gore might have become president of the United States. Democrats suggested that if Bush were serious about putting behind the bitter partisanship of the election, he would back away from his campaign promises and signal he was ready to deal.

  Bush's advisers, however, knew that would erode his Republican base before he got started. It would also signal that he could be bullied. One Bush adviser told a reporter, "Bush is a person who said what he believes. And it is important a president has credibility with Congress, so when they come to an agreement, it can be counted upon." That, the adviser said, was "why he is not going to abandon his agenda. He's not going to walk out and say 'I didn't mean it.'"

  Team Bush knew that it would have to make concessions along the way. The critical question was when, and the president's strategy was to stand firm first and compromise later, if necessary. "You lay out what your agenda is, then you see what points of agreement you can find," one senior Bush adviser said. "Otherwise you are signaling that what you say doesn't matter."

That doesn't mean that Bush is unwilling to compromise. Sadler explained that Bush followed his campaign promises with specific proposals. When legislative politics got sticky, however, Bush accepted compromises to get the bills passed. "At the end of the day, he knows what can pass and what can't pass," Sadler explained. "He will try to get as close to his proposal as he can, but in the end he will cut the best deal available."

- **Develop working partnerships via the "olive branch" approach.** Democrats in Congress were smarting over the election's outcome and were quietly muttering that the race had been stolen. They opposed most of Bush's campaign promises, like a big tax cut and a "Star Wars" defense system. They were in no mood to embrace a White House–Capitol Hill partnership. Bush launched a charm offensive. He met with leaders of both parties. He kept the meetings on time and he listened carefully, to signal respect. He showed patience and did not dive right into policy. He knew that charm would not change anyone's mind on issues of policy. But in focusing on style over substance, he worked to build civility—and a basis for future negotiations.

- **It doesn't matter whether you win by one vote or millions—as long as you win.** Pundits spent weeks after the election suggesting that the closeness of the election would hog-tie Bush. He chose simply to ignore them. The administration moved smartly and crisply to establish its policy agenda. They acted, in fact, as if Bush has won by

a landslide. That undermined suggestions of his power-
lessness and implicitly dared anyone to take him on.
Again, acting so helped make it so.

DEVELOP A PLAYBOOK . . . AND EXECUTE IT

After the inauguration, Team Bush faced cross-pressures on
what to do first—and how much to try to do. Democrats
wanted the president to focus on health care, especially
since reform of health maintenance organizations had been
one of the major pieces of unfinished business in the previous Congress. John McCain, who had been Bush's strongest
rival for the Republican nomination, pressed for campaign
finance reform. Bush and his advisers decided to stick with
the principal campaign themes and built an agenda of five
strategic issues:

1. **Education reform.** Over the last generation, federal officials from both parties have been increasingly interested
   in education, which has long been the province of state
   and local governments. Bush campaigned on the need to
   insist that local schools do a better job.

2. **Tax cuts.** When Bush took office, analysts estimated that
   the surplus would balloon to $5.6 trillion over the next
   decade. Rather than let Congress fund big increases in
   spending, Bush followed a course first charted by Ronald
   Reagan by laying out a plan for a huge tax cut—$1.6 tril-
   lion over ten years.

3. **Prescription drug plan for senior citizens.** A hot issue in
   the 2000 campaign, adding prescription drug coverage to
   Medicare was a top priority for Democrats. Republicans

feared that would swell the program's budget and worsen its long-run financial health. Bush advocated a new program of grants to the states to help subsidize the cost of drugs for seniors.

4. **Pay increases for military personnel.** During the campaign, Bush criticized the Clinton administration for allowing America's military preparedness to suffer. He wanted to review weapons systems, but first wanted Congress to increase military pay.

5. **A greater role for faith-based charities in delivering social services.** Although governmental social service programs were struggling, programs run out of churches in Philadelphia and Boston were producing surprising tales of triumph. This captivated Bush. For the "compassionate conservative," it was the ideal way to seek stronger social services without increasing governmental bureaucracy.

When Team Bush moved into the White House, the president and his advisers had a plan and they were ready to act on it. They knew the programs that would define the administration's first months. They knew how they were going to pursue them. They developed a playbook, with a theme for each week and, within each week, a theme for each day. They were developing their internal team and were building relationships with key players in the capital.

As columnist Franklin Foer argued, "The Bush administration is following its own kind of Powell Doctrine: Don't get drawn into situations where you aren't sure you can win."

Powell had used the doctrine to shape American strategy in the Gulf War, in Bush 41's administration. The lessons carried over to 43's presidency. Team Bush understood better than anyone just how difficult a job they faced in convincing members of Congress—and the American public—that the president was up to the job and deserved to sit in the Oval Office. But they believed that the only way to deal with the difficult situation in which they found themselves was to begin, carefully but firmly, with a strategy that could produce quick wins and strong momentum for other, harder steps to come.

RESPOND TO CRISES, BUT STICK TO THE PLAN

Generals know that war plans become obsolete at the first shot. Similarly, Bush and his aides knew they would have to adapt their strategy to shifting events. All presidents face unanticipated crises. In large measure, their ultimate success lies not in their ability to fulfill campaign promises, but in their skill in coping with the unexpected.

For Bush, the unexpected quickly materialized. In March 2001, Californians slid into the worst energy crisis America had seen in a generation. Parts of the state had such severe electricity shortages that power companies imposed "rolling blackouts," which shut off the power completely to consumers from high-tech industries to individual homeowners.

There was plenty of power around the nation. The problem, Bush and administration officials believed, lay in California's deregulation of the energy industry, coupled with a rapid increase in demand for power during the summer of 2000. There was plenty of electricity—just not at the rates that the deregulation strategy would allow the power companies to pay. The utilities ran out of money and the people ran out of power. Several Silicon Valley high-tech firms threatened to move to other states where energy was more reliable.

For the Bush administration, this was a big crisis. Night after night, stories about the blackouts filled the evening news. Their central strategic question: Did they have to act at all? Team Bush decided, in fact, to leave the tough decisions to California state officials. Bush asked Cheney to draft a national energy plan, which focused primarily on increasing energy production: oil drilling on federal lands, including Alaska's Arctic National Wildlife Refuge; fast-track regulatory review for building new power plants and transmission lines; and tax incentives for renewable energy sources. The emphasis on energy production was so strong that *Business Week* called him the "wildcatter-in-chief."

Environmentalists were furious, especially at the prospect of opening up the Arctic wildlife refuge for oil drilling. Democrats protested the secrecy with which the Cheney plan was prepared. Some western Republicans were unhappy that the federal government might override decisions made in the states. According to a Gallup Poll, 51 percent of Americans disapproved of Bush's plan. One Washington journalist pointedly compared Bush's energy plan with Clinton's health plan, released at about the same point of his presidency—with disastrous results. "If the President is not careful, energy could do to his Presidency what national health care did to President Clinton's," wrote *Business Week*'s White House correspondent Richard S. Dunham.

Like the unpopular Clinton health-care proposal, the Bush energy plan was put together in secret and contains certain elements that are strongly opposed by a vast majority of citizens.

Bush gambled that he could prevent California's huge energy problem from becoming *his* problem. He was worried that it would deflect attention from his tax cut and draw him into a big-government response to a problem that, by instinct, he believed ought to be settled by private energy developers. Bush knew that the Cheney plan would offend the environmentalists, but he did not count on being able to win their support in any event. A bit of luck helped—the California legislature found a way to finance more power purchases, and the headline-grabbing crisis ebbed away. In the end, he was able to sidestep calls for federal action, put his energy development strategy on the table, get back to the tax cut, and protect his popularity. His approval rating remained in positive territory—55 percent in a *Washington Post*–ABC News poll taken in early June. Bush's skillful move helped him avoid being drawn into a battle he didn't want to fight.

Team Bush barely had a chance to catch its breath before a far more terrible catastrophe hit: the terrorist attacks of September 11. Not since the 1962 Cuban missile crisis has a president dealt with a crisis as deep or as sudden. The terrorist attacks permanently changed the nation—and his presidency.

For Team Bush, the fundamental questions were who did it—and how to respond. With surprising speed, defense and intelligence analysts answered the first question by identifying Osama bin Laden's terrorist network. The second question was much harder.

For several days, the administration struggled to assess the threat and possible reactions. By September 17, however, in front of the smoldering Pentagon wreckage, Bush put the issue starkly. Referring to Osama bin Laden, Bush told his audience, "I want him—I want justice. And there's an old poster out West, as I recall, that said, 'Wanted: Dead or Alive.'"

A few days later he gave a rousing speech to a joint session of Congress. He demanded that Afghanistan immediately turn over bin Laden and said, "The Taliban must act and act immediately. They will hand over the terrorists, or they will share in their fate."

The U.S. response indeed came just a few weeks later, and the Taliban fell much faster than most analysts had predicted. To Bush's enormous frustration, there was no evidence that bin Laden died in the attacks or in the monthslong search that followed. But despite the failure to capture or kill bin Laden, Bush's approval rating soared. An October 9, 2001, ABC News poll put the president's job approval rating at 92 percent, the highest in history since polling on the subject began in 1938.

By at least that one very rough measure of success, Bush succeeded in quickly switching course and dealing with the terrorist threat. The question—the same one faced by John F. Kennedy in the aftermath of the Cuban missile crisis—was whether he could recapture the debate with the issues he had decided would define his presidency.

DEBATE, DECIDE—AND END THE DEBATE

In the months after September 11, Team Bush seemed to struggle to find its voice—and to reshape its strategy. Policy battles raged and new, unexpected issues surged to the forefront. The president either had little to say about them or, when he did speak, did not convey a clear sense of the administration's policy. Aides publicly voiced competing ideas about what the policy might—or should—be. Analysts and talking heads speculated about whether the administration's wheels had come off, whether the president had lost control of his staff and of the terrorism issue, and what the policy ultimately would be.

Reporters, looking for some edge in covering the story, parsed Bush's remarks for some shaded meaning from which they could deduce the forthcoming policy. From a distance, observers wondered if it was a deep pathology in Bush's management style, or whether that style was hard-wired into an approach that ultimately produced sharp policy and clear guidance.

After the Taliban was toppled in Afghanistan, the question was how the Bush administration would define the next stage of foreign policy. Would it focus narrowly on nation-building in Afghanistan, a prospect that ran against the president's 2000 campaign themes and his recurring criticism of Bill Clinton? Would it launch a broader strategy of engaging other nations in a global war against terrorism, even if that risked undermining the urgency of the effort by the inevitable bargaining with potential coalition allies? Would it try to shore up its relationships with Arab nations, or target states that seemed to pose the greatest terrorist threat? For weeks, speculation bubbled in the media. With his 2002 State of the Union address, however, Bush's famous condemnation of the "axis of evil"—Iraq, Iran, and North Korea—sealed the decision.

No sooner did the administration settle on this new strategy than turmoil in the Middle East boiled over, with Palestinian bombings in Israel followed by Israeli counter-attacks on Palestinian strongholds. Bush advisers believed that the Clinton administration had seriously overextended American diplomacy and credibility in its last months by trying to force a peace deal. They saw the Middle East as a morass, and they believed other problems—especially the "axis of evil"—were bigger, so they determined to keep their distance.

But as was the case with every presidency for decades, continuing turmoil in the Middle East forced the administration to act. But what to do? Should the United States try to force Palestinian leader Yasser Arafat from power? Try to nudge the Israelis from the occupied territories to create a Palestinian homeland? Get involved directly as peace broker or try to enlist a multination diplomatic effort? Different administration officials voiced different views, and some analysts suggested that the administration's "policy of the day" was defined by whoever talked to the president last.

Bush sent Secretary of State Colin Powell to the Middle East to try to broker a cease-fire, but Powell came back empty-handed. Vice President Cheney did no better. Bush decided to establish, firmly and unmistakably, his administration's strategy with a Rose Garden speech in late June 2002. He firmly called for the Palestinians to replace Arafat, hold new elections, and work toward regional reform. The speech did not solve the problem, but it did sharply define America's strategy. It also eased calls, from home and abroad, for a more active American role.

After the Middle East decision came fierce internal debate about administration policy toward Iraq. Bush had identified that nation as one of a three-part "axis of evil." In the months after his State of the Union address, administration officials focused on Iraqi president Saddam Hussein, calling him the world's most dangerous leader, rather than focusing on Iran or North Korea. They connected the Iraqi leader with the spread of terrorism, claimed that he was linked to the September 11 attacks, and argued that he had to go.

What to do and how to do it, however, were anything but clear. A blizzard of reports filled the media. Some stories reported that the United States would make short work of the Iraqi army. Others said it was likely that Saddam would lure U.S. forces into fierce door-to-door urban fighting through the streets of Baghdad. Some stories described the threat that Saddam's biological and chemical weapons posed—for American troops, for Israel, and even for America itself. Detailed war plans appeared in some newspapers, some purportedly from the Pentagon, though administration spokespersons repudiated them.

In fact, the stories appearing in the nation's most influential newspapers reflected the fact that the administration's hawks and doves were locked in a bitter internal battle. Vice President Cheney and Secretary of Defense Rumsfeld believed that the threat from Iraq was significant and that extended diplomacy would tie the nation's hands as Saddam grew closer to deploying nuclear weapons. Secretary Powell, supported by some members of the intelligence community, feared that a go-it-alone strategy would alienate the United States from its European allies and heighten Arab-American tensions, which were already high because of the September 11 attacks. It took little imagination to guess the source of most of the newspaper stories. They clearly were competing leaks signaling deep division within the administration, an administration that had earned its stripes on its no-leak policy.

The president publicly said little, except to repeat his condemnations of Hussein. Reporters again suggested that Bush's policy was adrift. In fact, some analysts pointedly asked whether Bush was fatigued by the nonstop intensity of post-September 11 events, was unsure about what to do, or perhaps had lost control of his foreign policy apparatus. The debates continued into Bush's monthlong August vacation. During that time, opinion pieces by old-time Bush family advisers Brent Scowcroft and James Baker sharply suggested that Bush was on a dangerous course. Analysts speculated that Bush 41 was using trusted former aides to send messages to his son, and to warn him off a risky confrontation with Iraq. As the administration moved ever closer to a confrontation with Hussein, a strategy for how to pursue the campaign seemed elusive and internal divisions seemed to rule the day.

The internal disputes and uncertain drift came to a halt in early September 2002. Bush and his advisers crafted a two-step rollout of a crisp policy. On September 11, Bush visited the sites of the terrorist attacks a year before. He gave an evening speech in front of the Statue of Liberty in which he said:

This nation has defeated tyrants, liberated death camps, raised this lamp of liberty to every captive land, . . . We have no intention of ignoring or appeasing history's latest gang of fanatics trying to murder their way to power. . . . Now and in the future, Americans will live as free people, not in fear, and never at the mercy of any foreign plot or power.

The next day, he went to the United Nations to throw down the gauntlet. He bluntly told the General Assembly:

The just demands of peace and security will be met, or action will be unavoidable. . . . And a regime that has lost its legitimacy will also lose its power.

Within the administration, Colin Powell and his allies had won a commitment to seek a Security Council resolution and international support for military action against Iraq. For their part, Cheney, Rumsfeld, and others ensured that the conditions for the UN resolution were high. Meanwhile, Bush and his aides worked with British prime minister Tony Blair, America's strongest ally in crafting the U.S. resolution in the UN. As the resolution worked its way through the Security Council, administration negotiators pushed hard to keep the basic policy intact, even as some nations—especially France and Russia—tried to soften it. The administration wanted a resolution that included threatening terms if Iraq did not cooperate with inspections, but had to settle for something less. Still, Bush won international support for the administration's tough position, including a provision forcing Hussein to disclose facts about his weapons program.

More than any other episode, the Iraq decision showed a recurring Bush strategy. Focus on one key issue. Allow aides to debate, and be patient if some of that debate spills over into the public arena. (Many previous administrations, Democratic and Republican, would have been apoplectic about such public airing of internal disputes.) Use the public debate to weigh the policy issues, gauge the alternative most likely to work, and assess the strategy around which political support was most likely to build. Set the course through a strong, firmly worded speech, in a venue that used the presidency's trappings to get as much publicity as possible. And then ensure that dissension ends and team members fall into line behind the new policy.

Other presidents famously pitched their advisers against each other to shake out the best policy. Franklin D. Roosevelt, for example, enjoyed tossing a tough issue to his aides and watching them battle. But few if any presidents have allowed such battles to be fought out in public, and for such long durations. Few demonstrated Bush's patience in allowing the issue to gel before deciding. Few have responded with such a crisp decision—and few have enforced such strict discipline after the fact to shut down further leaks and public debate.

Could a manager or CEO implement such a strategy? The answer is, it depends—on the situation, the organizational culture, and other factors. Corporations are not democracies—any more than the way presidents run the White House. However, organizations have become more democratic in recent decades. There is nothing wrong in permitting debate in an organization, at least for a set period of time. This can let the CEO (or manager) know where others stand on an issue. It can also give people the feeling that their voices will be heard. But don't forget the key lesson: Make a final decision to end the debate on a definitive note so the organization can move forward. Otherwise, the ongoing debate risks spilling out over subsequent issues and ruining any chance for cohesion around the basic strategy.

YOU'RE ONLY AS GOOD AS YOUR LAST VICTORY

Like all presidents, Bush learned important Washington lessons: Success lasts only until the next crisis nudges it out of the way. The American public applauded his handling of the September 11 attacks by sending his approval rating into the stratosphere, but Middle East turmoil and corporate scandals threatened to shatter his agenda. Political success has always been fleeting, but in the lightning-fast news cycles of the 21st century, success can evaporate faster than ever before.

On the other hand, the best way to ensure future success is to build on past success. A president who can define his agenda—and then stick to it—is far more likely to stay successfully on track when events threaten to derail it. Among modern presidents, Bush was notable for the uncommon focus he brought to his initial agenda, for the way he pursued it, and, most of all, for how he hauled the strategy back to his driving themes despite hurricane-force crosswinds.

In his first two years, he had mixed success on his "big five" agenda items. He won surprisingly quick success on his tax cut, with a $1.35 trillion 10-year tax reduction signed into law in June of 2001. Democrats knew he was trying to pick up the Reagan baton and use the tax cut to clamp down on future spending. But Bush put the Democrats into a politically awkward position of accepting his plan or seemingly embracing higher taxes. That helped him win his first, signature victory.

Helping kids is a sure-fire strategy, and, not surprisingly, Bush's education bill won broad support among Democrats and Republicans alike. It required states to set high standards for educational achievement, with annual tests for children in grades three through eight. States had to prepare annual report cards for each school. Bush's military pay hike plan likewise won easy approval.

Two other top Bush agenda items, however, ran into serious problems. To help the elderly obtain prescription drugs at lower prices, Bush wanted to issue Medicare discount cards. Drug stores and community pharmacists, however, filed suit to argue that the prescription card plan would treat them unfairly, and a federal judge agreed. Meanwhile, the faith-based charity initiative ran into a fierce buzz saw. Some conservatives worried that the plan would funnel federal money to charities with which they did not agree. Some liberals charged that the plan would violate the constitutional separation of church and state. Congress couldn't agree, and the bill eventually died on Capitol Hill as terrorism swamped the agenda.

When crises occurred, the administration proved deft at skipping around them—as was the case with the California energy crisis and turmoil in the Middle East—or tackling it head on—as it did in the war against terrorism. Team Bush showed an uncanny ability to shape its strategy in a way most calculated to help it win.

BUSH LESSONS

- **The first steps give lasting signals.** Bush knew from his study of previous presidencies that many of his predecessors started off balance and struggled to regain their footing. He worked hard to develop and project a confident stride, in style and substance, because he knew that first impressions last.

- **Develop a plan—and stick to it.** Writing a plan is relatively easy. However, what happens when unforeseen crises arise and demand attention? Bush dealt carefully and decisively with the crises, but he never forgot the main points of his strategy and constantly returned to emphasize them.

- **Don't fight battles you can't win.** Part of Bush's success came from choosing fights he could win—and avoiding being entangled in those (like the California energy crisis and the Middle East conflict) where he wasn't sure he could succeed.

- **Never allow disputes among aides to simmer too long.** Bush showed remarkable patience in allowing his aides to battle each other through the media about the administration's Iraq strategy. When, in Bush's mind, the issue ripened, he stepped in, framed a sharp and clear policy, and put an end to the feuding. Strong strategies require allegiance from aides and a broader consensus from the public.

The Importance of Message

"I ... had the responsibility to show resolve. I had to show the American people the resolve of a commander in chief that was going to do whatever it took to win. No yielding. No equivocation. No, you know, lawyering this thing to death, that we're after them."

—GEORGE W. BUSH,

ON ADDRESSING THE AMERICAN PEOPLE ABOUT TERRORISM

He [George W. Bush] stays on message, and I think that really matters more than anything else. He seemingly does not tire of saying the same thing over and over and over again. If you ask me what time it is, I'm likely to tell you about the history of timekeeping and clock making, about the manufacture of timepieces and other forms of measurement, about the kinds of regulation put in place by the government. If you ask George Bush what time it is, he'll say, "I think Americans have the right to bear arms."

—FORMER TEXAS GOVERNOR ANN RICHARDS

IT IS ONE THING to have a strategy. It is quite another to convince others to follow it. There isn't anyone in politics who doesn't believe fiercely that their way is the right way (and sometimes the only way). Without the ability to persuade the key players—members of Congress, citizens, even reporters—that his way is the right path, the president risks being just one voice in a noisy chorus. To do that requires a clear message, great skill in delivering it, and the knack of keeping the message on track.

Presidents rarely speak directly to the American public. Prime-time television appearances, like Bush's speech on the evening of September 11 and his State of the Union addresses, are rare. Television executives are wary of surrendering valuable prime-time slots (and prime-time advertising) for presidential puff pieces, and presidents hoard their capital with broadcasters until they need to use it.

Even more important, however, is that the president communicates indirectly, with most of the public, most of the time. Today, people get their news in a myriad of ways, from the Internet to cable news shows to the network evening newscasts. However, some get all of their news from David Letterman and Jay Leno, albeit with a whimsical spin. Some people—though a declining number—still read newspapers. In each case, editors, writers, and producers decide what's news, how to portray it, and what people will see and hear. And, to complicate matters even more, presidents have to compete with endless distractions, from increasingly hectic work schedules to soccer schedules for the kids. What's important is this: Strategies are worthless unless the message gets out.

MANAGE THE MEDIA

In other words, the president must struggle to be heard and, when he's heard, to make sure that what people are hearing is what he's trying to say. Some people—including presidential advisers—cynically call this "spin," but the simple fact is that communicating a clear, consistent, digestible message is a difficult feat. So many diversions compete for citizens' attention, and so many forces can distort the message, that communicating the president's message is extraordinarily difficult. At the same time, it's hugely important.

Some things make that job easier. White House officials often refer to the press corps covering the president as "the zoo." They often view them as dangerous wild animals who might snap at any moment, who must be carefully caged and properly fed. The press corps gets its news through a regular diet of briefings in the White House press room, a crowded and somewhat dank space above what used to be the White House swimming pool, where John F. Kennedy swam laps to exercise his back. Reporters in the room have assigned seats. The briefings happen at regularly scheduled times, and the routine gives the White House a home-team advantage.

Television reporters have assigned spaces on the West Wing lawn. They seem to be standing alone on the lawn with the beautiful backdrop of the North Portico behind them, but the TV images disguise how tightly packed in they are. When the president travels, reporters and film crews are kept safely behind a rope line, and the president's press secretary carefully doles out their perks, from scoops and leaks to private presidential interviews. The reporters who receive most favored status are those whom the president most prefers. The White House media team can carefully stage events to provide attractive backgrounds and good leads for news stories. The Rose Garden provides a great setting for bill signings, and few television backdrops are better than the Oval Office.

What reporters most want is a good story. What the White House most wants is for *its* story to get out. Skillful White House press secretaries use the former to get the latter.

All presidents know this and try this. Few have succeeded as well as Team Bush. The administration succeeded because it put a high premium on controlling not only the setting, but also the structure of discussions. For example, as counted by Martha Joynt Kumar, in his first two years as president, George W. Bush held substantially fewer press conferences than his immediate predecessors: W held 36 press conferences in his first 21 months, compared with 73 for Clinton and 61 for Bush 41.

When Bush does hold a press conference, his style is completely different from those of his predecessors. In the Reagan administration, reporters speculated that women who wore red suits were more likely to stand out from the crowd and get a presidential nod.

As explained by Francine Kiefer, during the Clinton years, some reporters tried a "bumblebee" approach, wearing a bright yellow pantsuit with black buttons, for instance, to attract attention. They believed that the first reporter standing had the best chance to ask the next question.

By contrast, Bush has staged his few press conferences with little advance warning. The strategy not only gave reporters no chance for a wardrobe switch, it also ensured that the White House could better control the flow of the questions. The president accepts no interruptions as reporters scramble to ask the next question. Bush and his team relentlessly work to ensure that the public hears their stories their way.

His staff have made fewer "senior administration officials" available for background briefings on the details of policy issues, and Bush has insisted that his aides and cabinet officials not develop back channels with reporters. In addition, reporters asking questions that senior officials considered "out of bounds" have complained that they've been frozen out of news briefings. For example, one reporter probing the behavior of the president's daughters found herself on the sharp end of a White House warning and quickly learned not to press too hard—or risk losing access to important sources.

The administration's openness, or lack of it, narrowed even more after September 11. Administration officials said they could not answer many questions because of national security concerns, but reporters complained that this was simply another smoke screen that the administration was exploiting for its own benefit.

At the center of the White House media team is Bush's acerbic press secretary Ari Fleischer. John Roberts, senior

CBS News White House correspondent, noted (half admiringly, half unhappily) that Fleischer has the uncanny ability to suck information out of a room. He doles out his daily press briefings with great finesse, sticking to his message and typically repeating the same phrase over and over again to make sure it's the one reporters use. Reporters continually prod him to say something controversial—and newsworthy—but he seldom takes the bait.

To restore decorum in the often raucous press room—and to prevent difficult questions from building momentum—Fleischer calls on reporters row by row. Since many reporters are working on different stories, their questions might go in dozens of different directions. Fleischer's message does not. CBS News correspondent Bill Plante, who has reported on the White House since 1980, complained that "in this administration, the controls on information are tighter than in any other one I have covered."

PACKAGE THE STORY, FEED THE ZOO

Fleischer's predecessors admire his disciplined focus on the message. Michael D. McCurry served as Bill Clinton's press secretary, and he often faced wild skirmishes with reporters trying to uncover juicy details amid the investigations into the president's behavior. McCurry believed that Fleischer might well have discovered the key to dealing with the White House press corps, which is "to be very, very disciplined and treat the press like caged animals and only feed them on a regular schedule."

The strategy worked for the president, and the media had little choice but to tolerate it. As Bob Schieffer, host of the CBS interview show *Face the Nation*, put it, "This is not an administration that's interested in a happy press. . . . What they're interested in is getting their message across."

One sign of how successful the Bush administration has been in managing the message is its skill in creating news events. Every occasion is a media event. Every media event is carefully choreographed to frame and emphasize the administration's message. For example, at some events, Bush speaks in front of a large banner that subtly repeats the same message over and over: "compassionate conservative," "reformer with results," or "no child left behind." Since no serious White House reporter can avoid a major presidential event, there is almost no way to edit out the message. No matter how editors or reporters might choose to write the story, the message of the day is there for everyone to see. The same message, constantly repeated, tends to get through, relatively unfiltered by the media.

Ronald Reagan was the "great communicator." Bush 41 was not nearly so polished, but he did win respect for his solid bearing in office. Bill Clinton loved the camera and it loved him. His aides grew increasingly polished at creating media-ready events. Despite George W. Bush's limited oratorical gifts, no presidential team has been so effective at framing a message, refining that message to its essence, repeating the message until it got through, and using the media so effectively to talk to the American people—and the world.

The lesson from Team Bush is clear. *Managing depends on message.* Whether you are the commander in chief or an executive of a large corporation, messages matter a great deal. They set the tone in an organization, help to establish priorities, and play an essential role in an organization's success. The moral for CEOs is: Make sure there's a mechanism in place for you and your management team to get your message out. And don't be afraid to repeat that message at every opportunity. Given the tremendous noise surrounding all communication, it's hard to emphasize the message too much.

HAVE A STORY—AND STICK TO IT

The disciplined message starts with the president himself. As he showed in the 2000 presidential campaign, to the surprise of his critics, Bush develops a theme and sticks to it. He rarely allowed himself to be distracted from his principal themes, and he relentlessly hammered away at his basic message.

In his surprisingly successful 1994 gubernatorial campaign, Bush seized on a handful of big issues—welfare, juvenile crime, education, and tort reform. He repeated them constantly and rode the message to victory. From that experience, he learned an important lesson about the "vision thing" that so troubled his father. Bush defines a message, repeats it, and hammers it home.

Some of that discipline comes from his personal style. Some comes from Karl Rove's laserlike vision of how to keep his man on track. And some of it comes from a painful lesson during the 2000 campaign. Sam Attlesey, a reporter from the *Dallas Morning News* whom the Bush campaign regarded as friendly, asked a question that seemed innocuous enough at the time: "Could you pass the White House security clearance as it relates to drugs?" Dogged by suggestions of drug use throughout the campaign, Bush curtly replied, "I've answered that kind of question already."

Bush media adviser Mark McKinnon worried that the answer would seem hypocritical—that other White House employees would be required to answer a question that Bush refused to answer himself. So Bush followed up with a phone call to Attlesey and said, "If you're asking me if I've done drugs in the last seven years [the period covered by the White House security clearance form], the answer is no."

Bush's cryptic answer invited a flood of follow-up questions and let loose an avalanche of stories. The governor addressed only the last seven years, which only dredged up more questions about the years before that. Was he high when he was flying a National Guard jet? Did his partying days as a youth include drug use? For a few days the issue threatened to swamp the campaign. But Bush's relentless refocus on the basic themes helped the story fizzle and avoided continued questions that could have unhinged the Bush campaign.

From that point on, access to candidate Bush was tightened. His advisers focused sharply on the messages they chose, and worked to make sure that reporters covered the stories they wanted to get out. Some advisers worried that tight management of the message robbed the campaign of one of its greatest assets—Bush's easygoing, charming way with voters. But the staff concluded it was better to put that asset at risk than to risk going off the track completely. The Bush team worked hard to manage the media carefully. They christened campaign press secretary Karen Hughes "Nurse Ratched," the crotchety former army nurse who ran the psychiatric ward in *One Flew over the Cuckoo's Nest* with unyielding ruthlessness.

FIND YOUR OWN VOICE
WHEN STEERING THROUGH CRISES

No matter how hard any president tries, staying consistently on message is impossible. Reporters live to be fed, and they're also constantly on the prowl for fresh tidbits not dished out by their White House keepers. Old issues come up in new ways. New issues intrude. Problems crop up that don't fit the message. And crises emerge that inevitably take both the White House and the capital press corps away from the preplanned presidential agenda.

Not only do crises strain the strategy, they also challenge the president's ability to speak to Americans. When events suddenly intrude on the president's agenda, they bump the president's message from the front pages. Responding to crises can require a whole new strategy. It also demands that the president reassure the public and build support for the new plan.

On September 11 these tasks challenged Bush in a way he had never been tested. The plane crashes in New York, Virginia, and Pennsylvania obliterated the president's education agenda. Citizens wanted to know what had happened, who had done it, what the president was going to do, and how another attack could be prevented. Perhaps most of all, they needed soothing from the nation's leader and reassurance that the government was in firm hands. His advisers told him that his first responsibility was ensuring the continuity of government, so he was shuttled across the country to a secure Air Force base in Nebraska. By late afternoon, however, he concluded that delivering the message of soothing, reassurance, and determination required him to return to Washington on Air Force One so he could address the nation from the Oval Office.

His speech was most noteworthy because it was made from the White House. His advisers candidly admitted later that they had not yet found the right approach and the right tone. That was a very tall order, given the overwhelming tragedies of the day and the fact that the president's aides had either spent the day with him flying around the country, had dug into the White House bunker, or had evacuated the White House complex completely.

Within days Bush developed his signature line: "Wanted: Dead or Alive."

Some analysts and allies—including his wife Laura—wondered if it made him seem too much a Wild West cowboy, but it was the perfect television news sound bite: short, punchy, and delivered with unmistakable firmness. He borrowed another good sound bite that Ronald Reagan once used in warning terrorists: "They can run but they can't hide."

By the time he addressed a joint session of Congress, however, Bush's speechwriters had to find the right words, and Bush had to discover the right "voice" to deliver them. The speech was a huge challenge. Bush was never known as an orator. His plainspeaking tone did not easily fit ringing rhetoric, and complex sentences did not play to his plainspeaking strengths. His down-home style sometimes did not sync with the seriousness of the issues. And he had to prepare the speech with far less lead time than was usual for such a major address.

During the weekend after September 11, Bush told Karen Hughes that he was thinking about making the address, but that he wanted to see a draft of the speech before deciding. Time was short, and one morning, he decided that he wanted the draft before 7:00 that evening.

Speechwriter Michael Gerson later said "I told Karen it couldn't be done. But Hughes had already told the president the same thing. Bush replied simply that "he didn't care." Against all odds, Gerson completed the draft on time, and it became the foundation for the speech that helped change the administration.

On such occasions, presidents have occasionally been drawn into melodramatic or incendiary language. The London *Observer* put the challenge crisply: Bush "walks a high wire between the expectations he has raised in a country prepared for war and what he can deliver in the world and on the ground." The president had to balance the need to "lift America's affronted spirit while, at the same time, spearheading a complex and demanding international effort against a mercurial global foe."

For his speech, Bush chose a tough, resolute tone that made unmistakably clear his intent to stop terrorists in Afghanistan. He was folksy enough to connect with the American people, yet deft enough in dealing with the nuances of international relations to talk to his global audience. Many observers believed it was the speech of his life. (Bush jokes that *every* speech seems like the speech of his life.)

What made the speech work was that the message fit the problem—and that the speech fit his style. It's one thing to write a ringing piece of rhetoric. It's more difficult to do so in a way that frames the right balance between subtlety and firmness in policy. It is most difficult to accomplish both while finding the words that sound and feel right. To be effective, a speech has to fit a leader like a perfectly tailored set of clothes.

Speechwriter Michael Gerson explained, "The president wants, in his speaking, action and directness, and he communicates that sense of momentum with clear outlines and short sentences." But organization alone isn't enough. "All that said," Gerson continued, "the president also demands an element of elevation in his speeches, that shows some continuity with the great traditions of American political rhetoric." Bush wants words "that challenge the country to its better self, or that talk about its deepest values, or relate to some great moral purpose."

With Bush's speech to the joint session of Congress, he found a way to tailor and wear those clothes in a way that had eluded him in the past. A new era in the Bush message machine had begun.

GET BACK ON MESSAGE
(EVEN IF EVENTS PULL YOU OFF)

After September 11, Team Bush faced a twin challenge: fighting the war on terrorism while getting back to the administration's original goals. The January 2002 State of the Union Address, with its focus on the "axis of evil," helped to accomplish part of this goal. The president suggested that the "axis" nations were involved in terrorism and that, therefore, an effective antiterrorism campaign required them to change their ways.

That provided a bridge on the international issues, but getting back to the domestic issues proved more difficult. The administration tried to bring back its effort to privatize social security, and it explored several prescription drug measures. But soon another crisis emerged, this one—Enron—hitting disastrously close to Bush in Texas.

By 2000, Enron had established itself as the sixth-largest energy company in the world. Revenues had doubled from the year before, and the company proudly put its name on the new baseball stadium in downtown Houston. Enron chairman Ken Lay—nicknamed "Kenny Boy" by his old friend, George Bush—had not only led the effort for the

company to buy naming rights, he also helped raise substantial support for building the new stadium. It was the
symbol of the company's leap to international prominence
and the leadership of Texas in the energy business.

By October 2001, however, warning signs were every-
where. Wall Street analysts were asking for detailed financial information, and the company announced it was taking
more than $1 billion in charges against third-quarter earn-
ings. The federal Securities and Exchange Commission
launched a formal inquiry into suspicious partnerships.
Disclosure reports revealed that the company had made a
$50,000 donation to the Republican Majority Issues
Committee, and the gift fueled political as well as financial
inquiries into the company's operations. Rival company
Dynegy explored buying Enron, but the deal collapsed in
late November. By December 2, Enron filed for bankruptcy.

For Bush, it was a nightmare. Enron's collapse meant the
loss of thousands of jobs in his home state. Moreover, the
political links to Republican officials—and Lay's close personal ties to Bush—sparked investigations. Bush had run
for office as a president who would restore integrity to the
White House. The collapse of Enron, involving friends and
financial misdealing, undermined that pledge. It also fed the
suspicions of some critics who had long believed that Bush
was too closely tied to corporate America in general and to
the oil industry in particular. When the General Accounting
Office filed an unprecedented lawsuit against Vice President
Cheney two months later, which suggested that Enron officials had exerted undue influence over Cheney's energy task
force, the suspicions began to stick.

The problem escalated with a string of other corporate col-
lapses and investigations in the first half of 2002.

Telecommunications giant WorldCom started hemorrhaging money and jobs. Standard & Poor's downgraded the company's debt to junk bond status and removed it from the S&P 500 index in May. The company scrambled to win new financing from its banks, only to announce in late June that it was firing its chief financial officer. An investigation uncovered $3.8 billion in expenses that had been improperly accounted for since early 2001. The loss prompted the company to eliminate 17,000 jobs, one-fifth of its work force.

Spurred by the constant stream of bad financial news, from Enron and WorldCom as well as other companies, the stock market continued its downward spiral in 2002. The year had little but bleak economic news, with a sluggish recovery that produced few new jobs. Columnists repeatedly warned that Bush 43 was sliding toward the fate of Bush 41: gaining a huge public support rating from foreign affairs, only to have a weak economy push him to political disaster.

No one saw the risks more clearly than Karl Rove. In January 2002, Rove received warnings from the administration's pollsters that Enron was a much bigger story than anyone in Washington realized.

Research then, and throughout the year, was clear. The president's personal popularity was high because of the way he dealt with September 11. If voters focused on terrorism and foreign policy, Bush would remain popular and his fellow Republicans would do well in the fall midterm congressional elections. On the other hand, if Enron, WorldCom, big business failures, and the plunging stock market dominated public opinion, Bush would be in a heap of trouble, which would likely result in the Republican loss of seats in both the House and the Senate in the midterm election.

For most of the year, Rove kept the spotlight on foreign policy. The president's foreign policy team had long since concluded that Iraq had weapons of mass destruction and that they constituted a genuine threat. During the summer, the administration's planners debated the options, and the unmistakable hint was that war would come in early 2003 if Hussein refused to be disarmed. The president made that point clear in his September 12 speech to the United Nations, and the administration kept up the Iraq drumbeat. He told the delegates:

If we meet our responsibilities, if we overcome this danger, we can arrive at a very different future.

The administration was especially skillful in keeping the focus on Iraq and off the sagging economy. As Congress returned to Washington from its summer recess on September 4, the Dow Jones industrial average dropped 355 points. The next day, however, newspapers headlined Bush's plans to press his Iraq case with key lawmakers. Every time economic issues threatened to swamp the foreign policy strategy, the administration arranged interviews, background briefings, and carefully orchestrated meetings to bring the focus back to Iraq. Foreign policy advisers talked about the dangers that Saddam Hussein posed and the risks that weapons of mass destruction could bring. Team Bush pressed the foreign policy message by repeating it over and over again.

Several highly publicized arrests of corporate executives helped defuse the scandals issue. Agents hauled away executives from Tyco International and ImClone Systems in televised "perp walks." They handcuffed and hauled away the founder of Adelphia Communications, along with his sons, on charges that they had used the company's finances as their "personal piggybank." The head of the investigation told reporters that the arrests sent "a clear message to corporate wrongdoers that handcuffs and a jail cell await those who violate the trust placed in them."

Bush himself put it sharply:

> *It should be clear to every shareholder, investor, and employee in America that this administration will investigate, arrest, and prosecute corporate executives who break the law.*

The drumbeat of corporate scandals had threatened to squeeze the administration's agenda—and, especially, its Iraq initiative—out of the public debate. By defusing the scandals and repeating the foreign policy theme, the administration got the debate back on track and refocused attention on the message it preferred. In fact, over just a few months, Bush changed the public debate on Iraq from *whether* to invade to *how*, *when*, and *under what conditions* an invasion would be most successful.

LISTEN TO THE POLLS,
BUT DON'T BE RULED BY THEM

In his campaign, Bush pledged not to govern based on polls. He said he was going to govern on principle, not on the findings of public opinion polls and focus groups. The promise was a barb at Bill Clinton, who polled more than any president in history, both to define his agenda and to shape his message. Cynics used to suggest, only half jokingly, that Clinton's position on any issue was whatever 60 percent of Americans believed. His pollsters explored what vacation spot and which family pet would garner the most support by voters.

Pollsters are not popular. They call people at mealtimes and, if they manage to get anyone to stay on the phone, ask probing questions. Citizens cynically (and correctly) suspect that politicians constantly use polls to spin issues. As columnist Joshua Green concluded, "One of the most dependable poll results is that people don't like polling."

Bush's promise to back away from polling was indeed a clever strategy—people don't like them—and a central part of his message—I'll do what's right. He sensed that people wanted leadership, and that they would not take kindly to a new president who tried to lead by the numbers.

A *Washington Monthly* survey of the administration's polling operations found that Team Bush, in fact, relied heavily on polling. However, they did not rely on them as heavily as the Clinton administration, and they relied on them for different purposes. During the first year, the survey found that Bush pollsters spent about $1 million, about half what Clinton's pollsters spent. Clinton used polls to position himself on the issues the public was most likely to support. By contrast, Bush set his strategy and then used polls to determine how best to sell his positions. As political scientist Lawrence R. Jacobs explained, "there's a lot more polling on spin," on how best to present the message that the president has already chosen.

For example, in February 2002 the Bush administration launched its effort to privatize social security. The president's speech focused on "retirement security," not "social security." He repeatedly used words like "choice," "com-

pound interest," "opportunity," and "savings." The phras-
es had tested well in polls and focus groups, and the president's speechwriters used them to craft a message in the way
most likely to sell. Moreover, Bush personally paid less
attention to the polls than did Clinton. Bill Clinton con-
sumed polls and could not get enough of them. He read
them and dug deeply into the results. Bush, in contrast, delegated the job to his political operation, led by Karl Rove,
who was charged with summarizing and digesting the findings. Poll results rarely surface in meetings with the president or senior aides. The political staff keeps tight rein on
the process and its results, and the president's pollsters
guard the fact that they work for him.

Analysts have debated both sides of Bush's shift in
polling strategy. Bush allies argue that it is more honest—
and fundamentally more genuine—to decide policy sepa-
rately from polling, but to use polls to determine how best
to talk to Americans about the decision.

As *New York Times* columnist Maureen Dowd pointed
out, Bush critics argue that it was more cynical to use "the
black arts of the Bush polling operation" to spin stories.

Critics also contend that the Clinton polling operation
was more democratic since it sought to find out what
Americans wanted and believed, and then tried to accomplish it. Bush allies counter that it's the president's job to
lead by making the tough decisions, based on the best
analysis, and not to set policy adrift on a sea of public
opinion.

The argument reflects polar opposite views on the role of
leadership. The debate skirts the fact that the Bush polling
operation has served the president's agenda and his management style well. Its low-key nature, moreover, has helped

erase the finger-in-the-wind tone that always dogged Clinton's decisions. That supported Bush's management style as well.

Team Bush has almost always known what it wanted to accomplish. It projected that message firmly and consistently, with remarkably little wobbling. There has been little ambiguity that might have given opponents the ammunition it needed to push the administration off message, or that might have allowed reporters room to write a different story than the one the administration intended. Not only has the Bush administration proved remarkably adept at focusing its strategy and framing a message to explain it but the team has also been relentless in emphasizing and reemphasizing that message, in a clear and consistent way, which has kept the spotlight on the president's agenda.

LINK MESSAGE WITH DISCIPLINE

No matter how effectively a president might craft and sell his message, however, it is only as good as his ability to deliver results. In the end, that is how all leaders are judged. The public would immediately sense whether a message was just a veneer papering over policies moving in opposite directions—or in too many different tracks at once. This is as true for a president as it is for a manager or a company executive. Message is key, but it is only one piece of the leadership jigsaw puzzle.

For Team Bush, the message was the outside layer of the onion. The inside layer was discipline. The president insisted that his aides not only keep to the message, but also move that message consistently to products. That's how Team Bush scored so many victories against such long odds.

BUSH LESSONS

- **The medium really is the message.** Marshall McLuhan's famous work has become a cliché. But for executives, it could not be truer. Bush has mastered the art of using the media to communicate his message.

- **Use the hunger of reporters for a good story to hone the message.** Bush's media team has mastered the art of feeding the media beast. Reporters constantly bristle at the control that Team Bush exerts over what they do and how they do it, but that control produced unusual clarity of message.

- **The whole package makes the message.** The administration has used all the tools at its disposal to package the message and how it looks. That lessens the chance that the media can mediate or alter the message, and it improves the direct tie from Bush to the American people.

- **Focus the message by repeating it.** And repeating it. Team Bush proved remarkably successful at keeping the message focused—and in getting debate back on message—by a simple technique. Whenever the president or his aides speak, it's news. Repeating a message over and over again constantly reinforces what they have to say and provides little chance for the agenda to slide off message.

The Disciplined Chief Executive

"... we don't have a lot of last-minute scrambling.
He [Bush] likes to have trust in the process, that he believes
he considers every angle—and makes a choice."

—BUSH SPEECHWRITER MICHAEL GERSON

"This is a buttoned-down administration, perhaps the most I've ever seen."

—STEPHEN HESS, BROOKINGS INSTITUTION

ON THE MORNING OF February 7, 2001, Robert Pickett created chaos on the southwest side of the White House grounds. The Indiana man had fired a handgun, and that brought Secret Service agents and Washington police swarming to the scene. Tourists scattered as hostage negotiators arrived. Police negotiators demanded that Pickett put the gun down. When that failed, a Secret Service agent felled him with a single bullet to his leg.

No one but the gunman was harmed in the late morning incident. Vice President Dick Cheney was at his desk, but President Bush was exercising in the White House residence. Some observers later snickered that Bush was away from his post. But for the early-to-bed, early-to-rise president, it was scarcely surprising to find him at a midday workout. Exercise has long been the core of Bush's disciplined life, and in fact, it was the core of his change in life in 1972. "I was so out of shape," he remembered in a cover story for *Runner's World*, and he later remarked that it was his running regimen that played the key part in helping him to quit drinking and smoking.

EXERCISE TO BUILD DISCIPLINE

Bush exercises six days a week. Most of the time it's running—outside, if he can manage it; inside, on a treadmill, if he can't. On Camp David weekends, he runs a tough three-mile course in the morning before going on a two-mile walk with his wife afterward. If he doesn't run, he uses an elliptical trainer, stretches, and lifts weights. The White House outdoor track is short and the Secret Service's security worries keep him off the nearby Mall. Not being able to do longer outdoor runs at the White House is "one of the saddest things about the presidency," he's said. Running, Bush explains, relieves stress, helps him sleep, breaks up his day, and recharges his batteries. Most of all, "it keeps me disciplined," proclaimed Bush, who said he expects the same of his aides.

Bush is no slouch on the course, and it's transformed him into remarkable shape for a man in his mid-50s. His times range from 6:45 to 7:15 minutes for a mile. Following the September 11 attacks, he ran even harder, his times came down, and his weight dropped slightly. As Bush himself notes about his running, "I guess that's part of the stress relief I get from it."

According to Bush's doctors, his body fat had shrunken from 19.94 percent in 2000 to 14.5 percent in 2002. His resting pulse is an astoundingly low 44 beats a minute.

Like the Kennedy administration's physical fitness craze, Bush's devotion to exercise spread to many members of his staff. Former presidential counselor Karen Hughes upped her fruit intake and took up yoga. Adviser Mary Matalin went regularly to the White House gym to "pump a few Arnies"—bicep curls and tricep presses, named after Arnold Schwarzenegger—and then, as she put it, some "glute something" exercises (presumably for the gluteus maximus).

James Wilkinson, deputy communications director, quietly asked Domino's how many pizzas he had ordered. The answer: 96 in five months. He stopped the pizza, cranked up the running, and lost 17 pounds.

For Bush, exercise is more than just a strategy to maintain fitness. It is part of his sense of internal discipline. He believes it keeps him sharp and focused. By insisting on a tough physical regimen, he develops a disciplined approach to decision-making as well.

ON TIME, ALL THE TIME

All presidents have strategies. All work hard to follow them. Success in executing them requires finding a way to quickly adapt existing strategies to new world events—to keep those events from pulling the manager away from the principal goals. For Bush, the key to adhering to his strategy and message lies in his relentless discipline. Nowhere is that discipline more important than in Bush's penchant for punctuality.

Bush insists on starting meetings promptly and ending them on time. He doesn't suffer aides who arrive late. In Texas, Karl Rove once upset Bush by leaving a meeting to take a cell phone call. Bush promptly locked the door on him so he couldn't get back in.

Early in the administration, Karen Hughes received a presidential glower for being 10 minutes late for a meeting on social security. She told the president that she had been briefing the press on Dick Cheney's health; it proved a barely good enough excuse. Staff members are expected to be present and on time for meetings that start each day at 7:00 A.M.

The contrast with the Clinton years could not be greater. Meetings almost always started late—but it was hard to figure out just how late. On the other end, Clinton's intellectual curiosity pushed discussions into intricate details, and that played havoc with his schedule. When members of Congress came to the White House for meetings, they often had to block out at least half a day because the timetable was so unpredictable. According to a Democratic strategist who worked on the Clinton campaign, "The omnipresent feeling was confusion. We weren't at all used to the rhythm of executive leadership. The Bush team is."

In sharp contrast, House leaders Dick Gephardt and Trent Lott were stunned by their Oval Office meeting with Bush in the administration's first days. At this meeting, Bush was warm, but he spent little time on small talk. Instead, he worked briskly through the agenda. He listened as much as he talked, and when he listened he listened carefully. The meeting started and ended on time. The leaders were soon back in their Capitol Hill offices, stunned at the contrast with the typical approach of the Clinton administration. Bush's discipline included a new approach to members of Congress.

In part, this was Bush's natural politeness and instinct for courtesy. In the campaign, he pledged to return civility to the White House, and punctuality was part of his effort. But just as much, it was a reflection of Bush's personal discipline. He doesn't like his time wasted and doesn't want to waste the time of others. He believes in focusing quickly on the decision at hand, getting the job done, and then moving on to the next agenda item. For Bush, it's an important signal that he values and respects those he meets with. Keeping himself on time helps him focus on the key issues.

CALIBRATE THE "LOYALTY THERMOMETER"

All presidential administrations have problems keeping their team members in line. Sometimes it takes time for people to gel in their positions. Sometimes cabinet secretaries, who rarely are shrinking violets, speak out on issues they care about, even if their passions don't match presidential policy.

In a single week, Treasury Secretary Paul O'Neill suggested (in an unprintable phrase) that the administration's 10-year budget surplus projections were unlikely to materialize. That undermined Bush's case for his signature tax cut.

Secretary of State Colin Powell suggested that the administration would continue along Bill Clinton's path of strengthening relations with North Korea, which flew in the face of Bush's "axis of evil" policy. Health and Human Services Secretary Tommy G. Thompson said he was troubled by congressional prohibitions on fetal stem-cell research, even though Bush at the time approved of the law. Senior adviser John J. DiIulio, Jr. had tough words for religious conservatives, who had been strong Bush supporters in the campaign.

Such internal flare-ups, of course, occur in all administrations. In fact, such brush fires have sometimes erupted into something akin to nuclear warfare. For example, Ronald Reagan's secretary of state, George P. Shultz, and Secretary of Defense Caspar W. Weinberger had brawls that constantly tested the administration's policy—and regularly spilled over into the newspapers. CIA Director William Casey tried to get Shultz fired. In the first Bush administration, national security adviser Brent Scowcroft found himself, together with then–Defense Secretary Dick Cheney, pressing for a tough line when Saddam Hussein challenged an American oil embargo. Secretary of State James A. Baker

III argued for a softer, wait-and-see policy. Bill Clinton's secretary of state, Warren Christopher, found himself isolated in his campaign to tighten human rights policy on China.

Bush believes in hiring the best people he can find, even if they are smarter than he is. But hiring strong—and strong-willed—experts into the administration is a prescription for conflict. Even though Team Bush faced some of the toughest challenges of any administration since World War II, the public disputes proved short-lived, especially in comparison with the public brawls of earlier presidencies. Senior team members, like Chief of Staff Andrew Card, quietly reined in some aides who wandered too far off message. Sometimes the axe fell quickly and brutally, as in late 2002, when Vice President Cheney was sent to tell Treasury Secretary O'Neill that the president wanted his resignation.

The administration's reaction to aides who openly oppose a Bush position or wander off message is not really the point. The key lesson lies in the preemptory steps Bush takes to prevent this from happening in the first place. Discipline was first asserted by building the team, encouraging loyalty, and reinforcing that trait through close interactions. Bush's approach had a soft side, grounded in the easy fraternity-leader style he developed at Yale. But it also has a tough side, forged in gritty political battles, especially in his father's White House. George H.W. Bush asked Lee Atwater, a tough and acerbic political spinmeister, to run his 1988 presidential campaign. Atwater had worked for potential rivals, and George W. Bush wasn't sure that he could be trusted with his father's future.

Bush asked him, "How can we trust you?"

Atwater replied, "Are you serious?"

Bush answered him bluntly:

*I'm damn serious, pal. In our family, if you go to war, we
want you completely on our side. We love George Bush,
and by God, you'd better bust your ass for him.*

Atwater told Bush he had nothing to worry about, but
that if he was still concerned, why not join the campaign
and keep an eye on him? Bush decided to do just that, and
became, in his own words, a "loyalty thermometer." Aides
learned that when his temperature rose, they needed to be
careful. According to Chase Untermeyer, an old Bush family friend and personnel director in Bush 41's White House,
"Political professionals look upon candidates as the baggage they have to carry on their way to being famous.
George W. was there to remind the various prima donnas
that their main job was not to make themselves look like
geniuses. It was to get George Bush elected."

When he became president, Bush 43 ran his White House
the same way. Through a combination of charm and sharp
edges, of team building and tough discipline, he never
allowed aides to wander far from the line he required.

BUILD ON PRAGMATISM, NOT IDEOLOGY

Bush avoided appointing ideologues to key jobs, with some
exceptions—most notably Attorney General John Ashcroft.
Given the strong support of the Republican right for his
campaign, and the Republicans' long exile during the
Clinton years, that was no small feat. Leaders of the
Religious Right and conservative Republicans pressed ideological true-believers on the Cheney-led transition team.

Leading conservative intellectuals, like Paul Wolfowitz, found themselves shunted to second-tier positions, and big thinkers grumbled that it was a "NINA" administration— No Intellectuals Need Apply.

The pattern continued during Bush's first two years in office. When economic adviser Lawrence Lindsey resigned in December 2002, Bush replaced him with Stephen Friedman, former chairman of Goldman Sachs. Friedman has been active in the Concord Coalition, a group that had long argued for balanced budgets and fiscal restraint. Many key conservatives did not think he was the right choice. They argued that the primary goal ought to be reducing taxes to grow the economy, not cutting spending to balance the budget. But Bush insisted on Friedman. His advisers signaled they were willing to take the heat from the right to ensure that Bush had a team he felt comfortable working with. He could have avoided the right-wing challenge by picking an ideologue. He instead went with a pragmatist.

Almost all key Bush appointees were Republicans, but most were moderates. Nearly all of them had substantial practical experience as well as personal relationships with him. He brought with him trusted Texas hands like Rove, Hughes, and Allbaugh. He hired experienced governors like Thompson, Whitman, and Ridge. Roderick R. Paige became education secretary after leading the Houston schools. Powell helped lead the army to success in the 1991 Gulf War, and Rumsfeld returned to the Pentagon a quarter century after he had last been secretary. Some of Bush's nominees, such as Gale Norton for Interior and Spencer Abraham for Energy had previously held controversial positions, and Norton was considered by many an ideological choice. But only John Ashcroft, nominated for attorney general, was challenged strongly on ideological grounds, and Bush won that battle.

The triumph of pragmatism helped cement the Team Bush discipline. Bill Clinton had selected his cabinet to represent certain interests. Chosen because of their ideas and constituencies, they not surprisingly argued forcefully for both when issues came to the fore. That, in turn, often led to fierce internal battles that got in the way of the president's agenda. By contrast, Bush focused on getting the job done—and the job clearly was the president's agenda. His focus on pragmatic appointees also helped secure discipline. The job, not the underlying philosophy, drove debate.

PLUGGING LEAKS

The well-executed media leak is one of Washington's most highly developed art forms. Every presidency has learned to feed bits of stories to reporters, disguised as comments by a "senior administration official" or "an official close to the president." When a story is too hot for a leak from the White House, the administration will find a way for the story to surface from a cabinet department, making sure to keep the leak far from the Oval Office. And, some White House officials say slyly, if they want a story to get out, they simply tell it to members of Congress, for no tale ever stays quiet for long on Capitol Hill.

White House reporters live like animals in captivity, penned up in the press room or shuttled around on the White House press room. They survive on meals and scraps that the press secretary regularly feeds them—but they are always on the prowl for the behind-the-scenes tale that will separate their reports from everyone else's.

That's what makes the leak such an irresistible tool on both sides: the White House, which wants to get a story out without making it a "White House story," and the reporter, who wants the story no one else has. Reagan speechwriter Peggy Noonan, in fact, wrote, "The White House is the only sieve that leaks from the top."

Those same forces, of course, make the leak one of Washington's favorite tools for dissidents and hothead aides. Officials on the losing side of a White House battle can always plant a story with a friendly reporter. And since so much of the White House debate revolves around the news cycle—the phases of capital news and media deadlines—skillful officials can steer internal administration debate by stirring up discussion in newspapers, network news, and the ever-whirring cable news networks.

Everyone reads the *Washington Post, New York Times,* and other major newspapers. Key officials get the regular White House clipping collection, prepared before dawn every day by staff members who stay up most of the night. It's impossible to wander the corridors of the White House and the nearby office buildings without seeing CNN, Fox News Network, or MSNBC glowing on small televisions tucked into office corners.

The White House agenda revolves around getting the message out, but there is always fierce competition about what the message should be. Senior staff members work carefully to influence the media—and each other—through the press, and what's reported in the media tells them how the battle for voters' souls is going. It's scarcely surprising, therefore, that presidents and their key advisers have increasingly obsessed over how to craft the media message—and how to prevent unintended leaks from distracting attention from the president's theme.

In the first years of the Reagan administration, small leaks often turned into spewing gushers. Columnist Mark Shields wrote that Reagan had been victimized by an "uninterrupted flood of damaging leaks."

The tug-of-war among Reagan's own advisers produced leaks and counterleaks that added up to a picture of a president out of touch and a presidency out of control. Reagan himself finally responded with a blistering statement, "I've had it up to my keister" with the leaks.

Afterward, Chief of Staff James Baker ordered that only designated officials answer questions on certain topics. That calmed the leaks for a while, but the insatiable demands of the media for news, and of staffers for spinning a story their way, inevitably fed the process again. By the time Baker became secretary of state in Bush 41's administration, Washington reporters acknowledged him as one of the capital's master leakers. Similarly, during the Clinton administration the ongoing battle for damage control and the constant battles among staffers caused information to ooze from all parts of the administration.

Bush had seen the leak process firsthand from his role as a close adviser in his father's administration. He not only knew how the game was played, but also knew how to identify the leaker. From the administration's earliest days, Bush made clear he would not tolerate leaks. Every new president says that. Few have been as successful as Bush in making it stick. Everyone knows their precise role on the team, and "anyone who talks out of turn doesn't last long," as the Brookings Institution's Stephen Hess put it.

Although some Republicans compare George W. Bush to Ronald Reagan, the discipline of his staff more closely rivals the quasimilitary style of the Eisenhower administration.

The information discipline extended even to some battles with Congress. Vice President Cheney refused to divulge information about his energy task force to the General Accounting Office, the auditing arm of Congress. The administration has been stingy in responding to Freedom of Information Act requests. And some officials who crossed administration policy were handed their heads.

Mike Parker, who had once been a Republican member of Congress from Mississippi, was used to speaking his mind before colleagues on Capitol Hill. Bush appointed him to head the Army Corps of Engineers, and Parker told a Senate committee that the administration's budget cuts would have a "negative impact." He also told senators that he did not have any "warm and fuzzy" feelings toward the Bush administration. Budget Director Mitchell Daniels was furious. He forwarded the testimony to the White House, and Parker was told he had 30 minutes to resign—or he would be fired. The resignation was announced a week later.

The cohesiveness of the president's staff and cabinet helped caulk the ship of state and protect it from leaks. Donald Regan, Reagan's Treasury secretary, noted that "the Bush loyalists have done an amazing job." They have loyalty to the president, and the president reciprocates. The staffers "don't need personal flattery, and they don't need to have they egos stroked, and therefore they don't have to leak to show how important they are." For the administration's first year, leaks were virtually nonexistent.

Time magazine learned, in July 2001, of an internal debate over the patients' bill of rights, but Chief of Staff Andrew

Card worked quickly to ensure that the episode did not recur. In late 2001, when the president announced a new management agenda that affected the jobs of federal employees across the capital, none of the papers got the story in advance. The president's commitment to be leak-free has sometimes led to decisions withheld even from the cabinet members affected. The officers affected by Bush's decision in June 2002 to create a new Department of Homeland Security did not find out until just a few days before the announcement.

However, the president's staff certainly did not lose their taste or skill for strategic leaking. In August 2001, as Bush prepared to announce his decision on stem-cell research, stories constantly surfaced on whom the president was talking to, how deeply he was considering the issue, and how he talked about it with virtually everyone whom entered the Oval Office. Before then, many news stories had continued to portray Bush as an amiable dunce. The stem-cell stories portrayed a president who was thoughtful, careful, serious, well-briefed, and fair in sorting out the complex issues in the decision. Unintended leaks, meanwhile, were rare. David Gergen, the Reagan staffer who told the press in 1983 about the antileak effort, was impressed. Gergen said, "They run a button-up place."

Team Bush's determination to avoid leaks extended to Capitol Hill. Congressional staffers had been given classified information to support their investigation on the September 11 attacks, but some of that information found its way into the newspapers. In a bizarre circle, FBI investigators began interrogating the congressional staffers, who were investigating possible intelligence failures by the FBI. The FBI even suggested they might use polygraphs to determine if the congressional staffers were telling the truth.

The administration's antileak discipline, however, began to break down in early 2002. Following the terrorist attacks, the administration quietly began to rotate key officials to secret locations to ensure that government authority would be continued in case of further attacks.

The Pentagon considered creating an "Office of Strategic Influence," to create "disinformation" and other strategies of spinning public opinion in other countries. A leak of this plan quickly killed that idea.

Meanwhile, Defense Secretary Donald Rumsfeld was furious that reporters learned of intercepted al Qaeda messages suggesting that the September 11 attacks were imminent. Reporters learned that Arabic communications included comments that "Tomorrow is zero hour" and "The match is about to begin." Rumsfeld launched a broad inquiry into who leaked the information.

The summer-long debate about a possible war with Iraq led to a quick increase in leaks and counterleaks. Details about war plans began appearing in newspapers. Some stories suggested Baghdad would be the first target. Others said it would be held until the end. By some accounts, war would require hundreds of thousands of troops. Others said that a much smaller Special Forces attack could secure victory. "Reliable sources" suggested that war would not begin until the December end of Ramadan—but that it would have to start before the weather began to warm in March.

Some stories suggested that Saddam Hussein was sure to lure American troops into Baghdad, where they would face punishing urban warfare, while others argued that even elite troops would cut and run at the first sign of a serious fight. Comedians joked that Saddam Hussein had everything but an engraved invitation to watch the first cruise missile land—except that anyone reading the leaks and counterleaks would have a hard time figuring out what the strategy was.

Secretary of State Powell was pushing for a diplomatic offensive through the United Nations, to build an international coalition before launching war. Some hawks in the White House staff and in the Defense Department did not want to have to compromise military objectives to build an uneasy, unstable diplomatic consensus. Some military officers were uncomfortable about the risks of facing Saddam Hussein's chemical and biological weapons, and they were not eager to face urban warfare. The leakers were among Washington's best, and there was little doubt that the internal administration debates were being played out in the pages of the *Washington Post* and *New York Times*.

Bush was uncharacteristically quiet during the media offensives and counteroffensives. Some observers worried that he might have been overwhelmed by the complexity of the decision or that he was unable—or unwilling—to stop the public side of the internal debate. On September 12, 2002, however, Bush delivered a firm speech before the United Nations. He detailed Iraq's violation of a long string of United Nations resolutions, and he made it clear that if Iraq did not disable its weapons and change its regime, the United State was prepared to invade.

As it turned out, Bush was neither overwhelmed by the issues nor unwilling to decide them. He was sorting out the options and meanwhile was allowing the debate to play out in an unusually public way, especially for Team Bush. Once he decided, the leaks stopped and the administration's officials spoke with a remarkably uniform voice on a notably complex strategy. Bush has been compared to Reagan in style and Eisenhower in management, but in shaping his Iraq strategy he was more like Franklin D. Roosevelt.

FDR was famous for pitting his advisers against each other, allowing them to fight (sometimes publicly) among themselves, and choosing his policy from the process. He found that the disputes tended to surface the big issues and test alternative solutions. The strategy Bush announced at the United Nations took a page from the doves' book—he decided to give diplomacy a chance to resolve the crisis, and he allowed other nations the chance to join the process. But it also took a page from the hawks' book—he decided that, if diplomacy proved unsuccessful, the United States would take military action against Iraq and force a regime change. From the turmoil of the 2002 summer debate, Bush emerged with a crystal-clear strategy, and Team Bush fell into step behind it.

WORK HARD BUT TAKE BREAKS (AND THEN STILL WORK HARD)

If Bush imposes discipline on his staff and office, he does the same for his vacations. An August 2001 *Washington Post* survey found that Bush had spent 42 percent of his presidency at vacation spots—or en route to them—including Camp David, his parents' Kennebunkport, Maine, estate, or his Texas ranch. But those "vacations" have often been busy, even exhausting, affairs.

His daily security briefings continue, regardless of where he is. Teleconferences link aides in discussions on important issues. His exercise routine becomes more intense, with longer runs through open country. Like Reagan, he enjoys clearing brush at his ranch. But unlike Reagan, he has put his aides to work on the ranch as well.

In August 2001, Bush twisted the arms of some aides, in toasty 102-degree temperatures, to help him construct a nature trail through one of the canyons on his ranch. Bush also interrupted his 2002 summer vacation constantly for campaign swings to bolster Republican candidates and to help raise money.

Bush likes to play golf with his dad. The Bush family has a long golfing tradition. Number 43's grandfather, Senator Prescott S. Bush, also served as president of the United States Golfing Association. Number 43 is not nearly as good a golfer as his grandfather, or even his father, but he does share one characteristic with 41: speed golf.

In August 2002 George W. Bush raced around the course in two hours, 14 minutes. It was not quite as fast as the record of one hour 24 minutes that Bush 41 once set, but Bush golf is a wild commotion of swinging, putting, and racing from hole to hole in golf carts.

Bush's discipline is hard-wired into everything he does. After the admittedly wild days of his youth, he grabbed firm control of his life. He lives determined to keep it that way, from avoiding alcohol to aggressive exercising. That discipline carries over to his work life, and it became the backbone of his administration. He insists that aides follow the same pattern, with tough internal discipline and no external leaking—except when it serves the team's larger strategy. In the end, Bush's discipline and self-confidence are woven together into the very heart of his style.

BUSH LESSONS

- **Staff discipline begins with personal discipline.** From a tough exercise regimen to a regular sleeping regime, Bush believes that good managers have to stay in top condition to function effectively.

- **Discipline begins with respect.** People who respect each other show up for meetings on time, stick to the issues, and explore important questions. That respect, Bush concludes, breeds the discipline an organization needs.

- **Allow discussions—but don't allow them to simmer long as public disputes.** Bush learned from his father's administration how corrosive public battles among aides can be. He determined that his own administration wouldn't tolerate them.

- **No manager can be all discipline, all the time.** Bush programs breaks into his week and longer vacations into his schedule. Some of these breaks can be frenetic, in the Bush family tradition. But he's discovered what relaxes him, and believes all managers have to do the same.

7

Leveraging Assets

George Bush and several talented people around him have made the White House a power center in ways that I haven't seen in a long time—all the way back to Lyndon Johnson. That is a big statement.

—ROBERT S. STRAUSS, FORMER CHAIRMAN OF THE DEMOCRATIC PARTY AND LONGTIME PRESIDENTIAL ADVISER

In the past, those who foolishly sought power by riding on the back of the tiger ended up inside.

—JOHN F. KENNEDY

THE PRESIDENT'S JOB COMES with surprisingly little power. The chief executive's performance depends on the power the president can build—and keep. Richard Nixon discovered that truth the hard way. In just two short years, he went from one of the biggest electoral landslides in American history to a resignation in disgrace. Americans greeted Jimmy Carter's sincerity but found him weak in dealing with the Iranian hostage crisis. Ronald Reagan was lionized, not only by conservatives but by many Americans. And Bush 41 fell from stratospheric personal popularity during the Gulf War to an embarrassing electoral defeat by Bill Clinton.

What's the lesson? A president's power doesn't so much come from the office itself. Rather, presidential power comes from his ability to fill the reservoir of public trust and support, to draw down on it sufficiently to do important work, but not to drain it through missteps that undermine his standing.

It's a mighty tall order. And the order is even taller if the president takes office with the reservoir already dry, as was the case for Bush 43. Without an electoral mandate, without a presidential honeymoon, with more than half of the nation's voters having voted against him, and with almost everyone questioning his intelligence and ability, Bush faced tough odds. Add to that a Congress with a narrow Republican majority in the House and a 50-50 split in the Senate.

Setting a strategy, building a team, framing a message, and instilling discipline wouldn't be enough. Bush walked into the Oval Office with as tough a job as any president in American history, and he had to find the reins of power over the rest of the government if he was to succeed—indeed, if he was even to survive.

FOCUS YOUR POWER TO ENHANCE YOUR STRENGTH

Bush was no stranger to such a job, however. Longtime Texas columnist and wag Molly Ivins noted that Texas has a "weak-governor" system. In fact, she argues, not only is the governor not the most powerful statewide official—the office ranks fifth, behind the lieutenant governor, attorney general, comptroller, and land commissioner. Many observers would disagree with her ranking, but the simple fact is that the Texas governor has relatively little real power.

The state has hundreds of boards and commissions, appointed by the governor. The terms of their leaders often overlap the governor's term, so new governors can find themselves surrounded—outnumbered and outgunned—by the previous governor's appointees. Once appointed, most can't be removed. As Ivins pointed out, however, the job provides a bully pulpit from which the governor can speak—and try to lead.

Despite the weak powers, Bush became a hugely popular governor who was able to campaign for the presidency as a "reformer with results." In Texas, he built his power by tackling tough issues and building support for them. He took on education reform, pushed through a tough education standards package, and won an increase in local property tax homestead exemptions. Even when there was an easier way out, he fought for what he believed was the right thing to do, in both policy and political terms. For example, with his presidential campaign gearing up, the property tax relief bill lingering in the legislature, and the New Hampshire primary just around the corner, he continued to push for his plan—and won.

For Bush, not only was it a matter of pushing hard for what he believed in; it was also focusing carefully on the key issues. As governor, he said:

To be for everything is to be for nothing.

On education, he found that the state had 50 performance goals. When the administration began, "We had so many goals we had no goals," said former Bush policy director Vance McMahan. Bush determined to change that with Vision Texas, the state's strategic plan. The plan set a crisp vision for the state government: "We envision a state where it continues to be true that what Texans can dream, Texans can do," he declared. The vision was built on four core principles: limited and efficient government, local control, personal responsibility, and support for strong families. Bush used the vision to shape his policy, and aggressively pursued the policy to build his record.

In Washington, however, he had a vastly more difficult job. The presidency has greater potential power, but to use it, Bush had to transform his reservoir of power from a dry hole to a steady supply. He had to find a way to work with a Congress with a sizable number of Democrats convinced he had stolen the election. He had to steer an executive branch that had been in Democratic hands for eight years. He had to try to move the bureaucracy, which is a challenge for every president. Every new president faces some of these challenges. None of them in the last century has faced this daunting combination.

DON'T TAKE ALLIES FOR GRANTED

Job One was dealing with Congress. Without a working relationship with legislators on Capitol Hill, Bush would be a lame duck before he had a chance to start. Republicans were anxious to move their long-stalled agenda—and to restore the heady days of the Reagan presidency. Democrats were wary of the new administration's agenda items. With such narrow party splits—a nine-vote edge for Republicans in the House and a dead-even split in the Senate—there was no margin for error, on anyone's part.

Bush's initial strategy for dealing with Congress was the same one he had successfully used in Texas. One reporter called him "a world-class schmoozer" who built legislative success on personal relationships. His personal ties were legendary, and even Democrats admitted liking him—to the point that one Democratic legislative leader appeared on a 2000 campaign commercial to tout Bush's ability to work across party lines in the legislature. William Allaway, a veteran lobbyist, said, "He's the only governor I've ever known that I would like to have sitting on my back porch drinking beer and talking baseball."

Congressional Democrats were struck by the personal touch, and they greatly appreciated it. It was better than the right-wing hammer they had expected. They had also demanded that Bush back away from his more aggressive campaign proposals, especially for a big tax cut. They didn't get their wish. But the respect and personal attention that Bush showed gave them some hope in working out a bipartisan compromise for governing.

The strategy, however, soon ran headlong into serious trouble—not from Democrats, but from a member of Bush's own party in the Senate. In May 2001 the White House was stunned to learn that Vermont senator Jim Jeffords, a longtime Republican, was preparing to bolt the party and declare himself an independent. The defection would give the Democrats control of the Senate and pose huge problems for Bush and his agenda. Bush and his aides launched a full-force offensive to try to keep Jeffords in the Republican fold, but it failed. Back in Montpelier, the capital of his home state, Jeffords sadly said that the party once stood for "moderation, tolerance, fiscal responsibility." With Bush's election, he no longer believed that was true. Increasingly, he said, it had become "a struggle for our leaders to deal with me and for me to deal with them."

The White House was stunned by the announcement. By the time they launched their full court press to keep Jeffords, it was too late. Administration officials knew that Jeffords was unhappy, especially over earlier scraps about the first version of the Bush tax cut plan. But they had no idea that relations had soured to the point that he would bolt the party.

For Jeffords, the problems had been building to the boiling point. There were some small slights that loom large in capital politics—the White House had denied coveted tour passes to Jeffords's constituents, and Jeffords had not been invited to an event the month before recognizing the

Vermont teacher of the year. There were also important policy differences. Jeffords had long campaigned for increased funding for special-needs students, and Republicans in the Senate opposed his plan. The grievances gradually built up until Jeffords decided to quit the party.

While Bush aides, both publicly and privately, said that the defection was not a serious issue, it sent up red flags across the capital. Old-time Republican insiders were shocked that the administration did not have better intelligence about Congress, especially about a member of their own party. Some observers also wondered whether the defection revealed fundamental flaws in Bush's legislative strategy. Bush was indeed warm and charming with members of Congress, but critics warned that he had done little to build one-on-one relationships that could be counted upon in the crunch.

Behind the scenes, top aides, especially Karl Rove, played a ruthless game. He questioned Jeffords's motives, which enraged the senator, and some insiders speculated that Rove was conducting a revenge campaign against him. The combination—a president too breezy in person and a staff too heavy-handed in private—was a sign of serious trouble, especially to some Republicans. One congressional analyst said, "It was less political hardball and more juvenile T-ball."

As the team gained more experience in Washington's folkways, it became more practiced in holding the Republican base and massaging the party's moderates. That approach, in fact, proved pivotal in winning close legislative victories in 2002 and built up to the Republicans' congressional wins in the midterm elections.

The Jeffords story taught Team Bush an important lesson. As the administration was scurrying to build support among key congressional swing voters for the tax reform plan, aides neglected to nurture their Republican base. In the process, they lost control of the Senate and could have lost the tax bill. Without a strong foundation, ambitious goals can collapse. The lesson: Don't become overextended by neglecting the base while trying to broaden support.

"IT'S ABOUT CONTROL"

John Dean, Richard Nixon's White House counsel and no stranger to ruthless political maneuvering, noted, "This administration has been stiff-arming Congress." On homeland security issues, the administration has been reluctant to give information to members of Congress, and even when the information was shared privately, the administration has refused to declassify it so legislators can publicly discuss it.

That has led some members of Congress to complain that what they have learned in private has contradicted what the president says in public—but that they can't use what they know to engage the debate. When the General Accounting Office—the investigative arm of Congress—asked for records of Vice President Cheney's task force, the administration refused. As Dean argued, "not since Richard Nixon stiffed the Congress during Watergate has a White House so openly, and arrogantly, defied Congress's investigative authority."

Many of the administration's key members, especially Cheney and Rumsfeld, had previously served in Washington. They came to the Bush White House convinced that the balance of power had shifted much too far toward Congress. They were determined to shift that balance back toward the president, even if it meant ruffling congressional feathers. They thought that Congress was engaging in too much pork-barrel spending, which resulted in an out-of-control budget. They believed that too many national security secrets were leaking out of Capitol Hill. They were convinced that dealing with the new breed of national problems, especially terrorism, required a strong and effective president.

So the administration continued to play it tough. In the summer of 2002, congressional appropriators bundled money for homeland defense together with other items, including some the administration did not want. Bush's budget director Mitch Daniels argued that the spending was too much, so the president vetoed the entire bill—including money to improve the FBI's computer system and to enhance aid for Afghanistan. Bush agreed. "This isn't about spending," one senior administration official explained. "This is about control."

In politics, balance is key. Team Bush struggled to find just the right balance in the legislative-executive branch relationship, so delicately fashioned by the framers of the Constitution and ever shifting in practice. The president worked to provide just the right amount of stroking to keep a coalition together, but his aides did not hesitate to use a heavy hand when they thought the balance was off. They knew this might cost them some victories, but they were convinced their ultimate success—and the nation's welfare—required wresting power away from Capitol Hill in favor of the executive branch.

ACT QUICKLY, BUT LEAVE NO FINGERPRINTS

Team Bush sometimes played hardball in their relations with Congress, but sometimes they applied a deceptively deft and subtle touch. In December 2002, Republican Senator Trent

Lott threw the Republican Party into turmoil by appearing to praise the segregationist legacy of Senator Strom Thurmond at Thurmond's 100th birthday party. For Bush, the turmoil that resulted was a political nightmare. The Republicans had just stunned the Democrats by wresting away control of the Senate, and Lott was about to become the new majority leader. Bush was planning on using the new legislative session to ramp up his 2004 presidential campaign and broaden his political base. Lott's comments threatened to distract attention from the Bush agenda and undermine the president's efforts to appeal to moderate voters.

Bush could not afford to be seen pushing Lott out of the GOP majority position. Republican senators would resent being muscled that abruptly. But the last thing Bush needed as 2003 began was a wounded Senate leader, protracted criticism of the party's position on race, and an extended distraction just as the administration was framing its agenda.

At a speech in Philadelphia, Bush took the unusual step of criticizing Lott directly. "Any suggestion that the segregated past was acceptable or positive is offensive, and it is wrong," he told his applauding audience. That was Bush's last public comment on Lott. But for the next week, White House aides carefully eroded Lott's position. Through calculated leaks by "senior White House officials," the drumbeat continued. Secretary of State Colin Powell, the administration's senior African-American official, said that he "deplored" what Lott had said, and Florida governor Jeb Bush said that "something's going to have to change. This can't be the topic of conversation over the next week."

It wasn't. Within days, Lott announced he would remain in the Senate but step down as majority leader. James Carville, longtime Clinton strategist, admired the fact that "it was a clean extraction." Replacing Lott was Tennessee senator Bill Frist, which led Robert S. Strauss, former chairman of the Democratic National Committee, to note, "They've got a skilled surgeon coming in to run the Senate, and they used a surgeon's skill to remove Lott without leaving any fingerprints." He was amazed at the administration's skill. "Whether you agree or disagree with this administration on policy, you have to give the White House tremendous credit for coming to town and after two years having this kind of political performance."

It was a delicate hand to play. Push too hard and Bush risked offending the clubby traditions of the Senate. Not push hard enough and the Lott problem could have lingered, leaving Lott gravely wounded but still majority leader—or giving Democrats weeks of news stories that would wound Bush's legislative agenda. Instead, Bush acted quickly to ensure he didn't himself become the issue.

Bush's blatant support for Frist risked inserting himself too deeply into congressional politics, which threatened to cause trouble later. In the short term, however, he blunted the political uproar. With a deft touch, Bush solved the problem and more clearly cemented his position in Washington. It was a remarkably well-played hand—all the more for the team's ability to secure victory out of an unforeseen problem that could have proved to be a damaging, lingering sore.

USE INNOVATIVE TACTICS TO
MAINTAIN A COHESIVE TEAM

A president not only has the daunting job of dealing with 535 members in the two houses of Congress, each of whom has a separate base of power; he must appoint the 650 top positions in the executive branch. And these officials in turn choose about 2500 other appointees—for more than 3000 political appointments in all. Every decision is politically important, for there are more people who want key jobs than there are jobs to fill, and applicants inevitably believe they're more deserving than anyone else. In the 18th century, Louis XIV complained, "Every time I bestow a vacant office I make a hundred discontented persons and one ingrate." Things haven't changed much since.

Political appointees are critical to a president's ability to accomplish his agenda. Most of what happens in the federal government's far-flung operations—from rescuing boaters in trouble to putting out fires in the national forests—is under the control of managers throughout the government. The president and his advisers can, at best, focus on only a handful of issues at a time, and they cannot direct detailed operations in any area without neglecting most of the others. To keep government policy consistent, therefore, the president has to rely on his appointees.

The very forces that make these appointees so important to the president's agenda, however, make them hard to control. Presidential expert Richard Neustadt told Clinton's advisers during the 1992 campaign that if Clinton won, he needed to put his appointees into place quickly. But he noted that, no matter what the incoming administration might do, "In time they all go native anyhow."

Bush was determined to slow the loss of control over his appointees. Given the complexity of the president's job and the appointees' inevitable slide toward autonomy, that was a tall order. But the administration used money left over from the transition to try an innovative strategy—a Web site specifically tailored for presidential appointees, www.results.gov. Clay Johnson, presidential personnel director, said that the Web site "allows us to stay in the orientation and team-building business"—to continue the process of training members of the presidential team and, the administration hoped, to help appointees become more effective.

As Bush said on his Web site, "We're all here to make a difference—a big difference—to tackle big issues like creating economic security for all Americans, protecting the homeland, and strengthening our national defenses. Another issue that is critical to the success of this administration is the implementation of my management agenda. We're interested in results, and to be effective, we have to work together and learn from each other. This site will help us do that."

The site warns appointees, for example, about the dangers of "Potomac Fever," a dangerous disease characterized by "extreme disorientation, memory loss, and occasional delusions of grandeur." Words like "paradigm and synergy" creep into the speech of those afflicted with the disease. Other symptoms include a sense that "words like million and billion no longer seem so large," and a belief that the individual could be "effective if only OMB [the president's budget office] would loosen up on the budget strings." Those afflicted "may forget who appointed them to their position"—and "that they serve at the pleasure of the president." The site included handy tips on surviving Washington without becoming captured by it, and an introduction to legislative affairs ("Accept the fact that Congress is there, was there long before you got to where you are, and will be there long after you leave").

There was never a chance that the Web site would eradicate Potomac Fever or prevent the president's appointees from "going native." But by reemphasizing the president's message—and reminding appointees that they were members of the president's team—the president's advisers hoped to stop the disease's spread and promote more cohesion among the thousands of appointees.

FOCUS ON RESULTS

Team Bush reached out even more to tackle bureaucracy through an aggressive management agenda. The Clinton administration had attempted to "reinvent" government. Its downsizing movement, however, quickly stirred opposition among federal bureaucrats, and its effort to "empower" those officials never received much support in Congress.

Bush decided on a different approach. Where the Clinton government reform movement was run out of a small office distant from the center of West Wing power, Bush directed his management agenda from the Office of Management and Budget, the often feared and always respected voice of the president's budget priorities. Where the Clinton strategy worked to motivate employees to do more with less, Bush focused on measuring the results of government programs and then on using those results to drive budget decisions. During the 2000 campaign, Bush said bluntly:

Governments should be results-oriented. . . . Where we find success, we should repeat it, share it, and make it the standard. And where we find failure, we must call it by its name. Government action that fails in its purpose must be transformed or ended.

At the core of the Bush management strategy was the belief that if you grabbed bureaucrats by their budgets, their hearts and minds would follow. His team believed that the Clinton effort had fallen short because of his administration's failure to focus attention on key management reforms. Bush was determined to change that—to give federal officials "freedom to manage," but to hold them responsible for results.

The launch of the management agenda as part of the December 2001 budget process was a profound surprise, even to many members of the president's cabinet. They came to the Oval Office for the usual round of appeals—to ask for more money than OMB recommended and to protest programs that had been cut. When they met with Bush, they were amazed to find a scorecard of their department's track record on issues like financial management and human capital. The scorecard was a simple stoplight system: green for success, yellow for mixed results, and red for unsatisfactory. Only one agency—the National Science Foundation—got a green light. Most departments, including major agencies like Defense, State, Justice, and Health and Human Services, got red lights across the board.

The stoplights got the cabinet secretaries' attention. In the next budget review, OMB turned up the heat by forcing agencies to measure the results of some of their programs—and pledged to move quickly to force all agencies to assess the outcomes of all programs. "The scorecard employs a simple grading system common today in well-run businesses," the administration said. Team Bush was intent on bringing those business practices to government. Bush intended those practices, in turn, to help him increase his leverage over the federal government's vast empire of programs, agencies, and bureaucrats.

OUTFLANK CRITICS—QUICKLY

Both these strategies—rebalancing power with Congress and increasing leverage over the executive branch—came together in the president's proposal for a new Department of Homeland Security. In the aftermath of September 11, critics argued that the administration had fumbled over key pieces of intelligence that might have alerted officials to the attacks. Calls arose almost immediately for restructuring the government to cope with the new threat.

The Bush administration fought that argument fiercely. None of the key players—Defense, State, the FBI, and CIA—wanted to be reorganized, and each one had a powerful champion in the president's inner circle. Over the next few months, however, reporters discovered that before the attacks, two different FBI agents had warned that suspicious individuals were seeking flight training. A Minneapolis agent—Colleen Rowley, later named one of *Time*'s "persons of the year"—wrote a devastating 12-page memo suggesting that the field staff had informed FBI headquarters of their worries only to have headquarters fail to act. Rowley's testimony before a congressional committee was explosive.

Bush grabbed back the reins the very same evening with a startling announcement. After months of opposing a restructuring, and on the very day that Rowley testified, he proposed creating a new cabinet-level Department of Homeland Security. The administration's critics had long been arguing that the White House Office of Homeland

Security wasn't up to the job—that it was too little, too late. Fueled by Rowley's testimony, members of Congress were gearing up for a searing investigation into what the administration knew, when it knew it, and what might have been done. In a single stroke, Bush flipped 180 degrees. He pulled the debate back from what the administration should have done to what Congress now should do. And he made the case for restructuring the federal government's homeland security apparatus—on his terms.

The immediate consensus was that the creation of the new department would be a slam-dunk. No one wanted to oppose a proposal for improving coordination for fear of being blamed in case another attack took place. Some analysts floated alternative proposals for a more streamlined department, but inside observers suggested there was little chance they could pass. The consensus was that Bush's plan was unstoppable.

Indeed, Republicans and Democrats on Capitol Hill quickly agreed on the elements that would be brought together into the new department. The Democrats, however, raised a different objection. They were in favor of consolidating federal functions into a new department, they said, but objected to the management changes, permitting the president more flexibility with workers, that Bush had also requested.

Bush asked for the freedom to reorganize the new department, to reallocate funds, to override existing collective bargaining agreements, and more flexibility to hire and fire the department's workers. "President Bush's proposed Department of Homeland Security is an enormous grant of power to the executive branch," Senator Robert Byrd, the Senate's chief guardian of its powers, told CNN. "We must not cede this power—power the administration wants but not necessarily needs." Bush countered by saying, "I need the flexibility to put the right people at the right place at the right time to protect the American people—and the Senate better get it right."

The bill got hung up in interparty wrestling before the 2002 midterm elections. When the Republicans won back control of the Senate, Democrats realized they had little hope of derailing the Republican's legislative package. They quickly negotiated the remaining differences and created the new department. The irony was that the president, committed to shrinking the size of the federal government, had presided over the creation of a new department and a big expansion of the federal work force. In the end, though, Bush got what he wanted.

SHIFTING THE BALANCE OF POWER

Not only did Bush have an ambitious, if highly focused, policy agenda when he came into office. He also believed deeply that success depended on strengthening the office of the presidency. That was at the core of his management style. While policies come and go, he understood that shifts in the institutional balance of power often have far deeper and lasting impact.

At the beginning of his term, some people saw Bush 43 as a continuation of the presidency of Bush 41. Cartoonists and columnists found the dynastic theme irresistible. Some Republicans quietly hoped that the Bush administration would mark the completion of what they called the Reagan Revolution, launched in 1980, continued in the Bush senior years, and interrupted by the eight Clinton years. Bush's insistence on disarming Saddam Hussein, who had tried to have Bush 41 killed, fed the former belief. His initial tax cut plan helped confirm the latter.

But seeing Bush, in substance and style, as extensions of previous Republican presidents paints a muddy, shallow portrait of the president. He is very much his own man, with a policy agenda different from his predecessors and with an uncommonly disciplined focus. Terrorist attacks forced him to adapt the agenda to a suddenly different 21st century world. At the same time, he insisted that the attacks would not deflect long-range attention away from his fundamental agenda. He took up his father's campaign against Iraq, but he did so on more fundamental issues and with a willingness to go it alone if necessary. He has embraced Reagan's tax cut strategy, while pressing for more spending on and a stronger federal role in education, which fits the "compassionate conservative" label.

If Bush 43 has been his own man on policy, he has been even more his own president in style. He's been more disciplined in building a team and enforcing discipline, in ways reminiscent of Eisenhower's staffing. He has tolerated raucous debate among his aides, but then quickly shut dissension down when decisions were to be made, as Franklin D. Roosevelt did. He has been more focused in defining and keeping to his message. Most important, Bush has strategically sought to shift the balance of Pennsylvania Avenue power from Congress back to the White House. He has also tried to use the critical power of the federal budget to get the attention of the federal bureaucracy—to steer policy and control spending.

BUSH LESSONS

- **Power has to be built.** From his close observation of his father's presidency, Bush knew that the job comes with little reservoir of power. A president has to work hard to fill that reservoir in order to get anything done.

- **Target your effort.** Both in Texas and in Washington, Bush was convinced that too many goals were worse than no goals at all. A focused strategy was the keystone of success.

- **Broaden the base.** Many key players can make the difference in achieving the agenda. Discovering who they are and how to win their support—or blunt their opposition—requires a subtle combination of the tools at the president's disposal.

- **Reach deeply to engage all team members.** Winning loyalty from the inner team is one thing. Everyone sets their compass by the budget; using the budget to focus managers' energy improves the odds that everyone sails in the same direction.

TEAMING UP FOR THE FUTURE

Avoiding the Seven Deadly Leadership Traps

If I have erred, I err in company with Abraham Lincoln.

—THEODORE ROOSEVELT

My administration will continue to act on the lessons we've learned so far to better protect the people of this country. It's our most solemn duty.

—GEORGE W. BUSH, NOVEMBER 27, 2002

GEORGE W. BUSH AMAZED even his foes with his steady hand on the tiller. It was no secret that half the country questioned his legitimacy as a sitting president. Yet the responsibility for directing the response to the worst attack on American soil in more than half a century fell to him. He rode the roller coaster of the economy, including a huge stock market collapse and criminal charges against some of the nation's largest corporations and most powerful business executives. He charted a war against Iraq, strategized about the Korean peninsula, and tried to broker truces in the endless Middle East struggles.

Through it all he remained remarkably consistent. His style, honed in Austin, came to Washington with only modest fine-tuning. The George W. Bush we saw in January 2001 remained remarkably the same through the crises that followed. If anything, he became more confident in himself and more committed to his style.

However, it is the paradox of leadership that the seeds of failure often grow in the bounty of success. Why? One reason is that the more an approach seems to work, the more enticing it is to employ that same approach on all problems all the time. Moreover, it can risk blinding leaders to potential traps and unintended consequences. No style or approach can possibly fit every situation. Sometimes the approach that has proved so effective fails miserably when that leader is confronted with a different setting, issue, or set of circumstances. Bush's clothes fit him well, just as his style does. But there are seven traps that have the potential to trip him up and even cripple his presidency.

1. PAINTING EVERYONE WITH THE SAME BRUSH

People who know Bush report that his most outstanding feature is his easy way with people. He often teases visitors and mugs for the cameras. He was a prankster on the 2000 campaign plane and sometimes (literally) turned the cameras back on reporters. Engaged in arguments over policy issues in the hallways of the Texas legislatures, legislators sometimes were surprised when Bush snuck up behind them and put them in a bear hug. Bush's ability to connect with people in a warm and likable way has been one of his greatest strengths since his college fraternity days.

In the spring of 2002, however, the easygoing, fraternity manner landed with a thud in Europe. One British journalist dourly reported, "Like certain distinctive wines, President George W. Bush does not travel well." In fact, "those aspects of his personality that play best in Peoria play worst in Paris." The journalist noted that, in the three years he had covered French president Jacques Chirac, he never heard anything remotely like a joke. Bush, in contrast, thrived on them.

When Bush and Chirac appeared together, Chirac was visibly annoyed when Bush called him "Jacques," and their public uneasiness carried over to their private meetings. Bush's session with German chancellor Gerhard Schroeder went little better. Russian president Vladimir Putin was reported to have been none too pleased when he found out that Bush had nicknamed him "Pootie Poot," though the two did exchange friendly barbs on stage.

Overall, Bush struggled during his trip to Europe. His Washington social schedule, which typically ended at 7:30 (so he could get to bed at his usual time), didn't sync with the European dinners that usually went until midnight. He was visibly tired—and noticeably grumpy. He did run on the treadmill that was especially installed on Air Force One for the trip, but that didn't help much. His Texas way and early-to-bed/early-to-rise routine didn't match European sensibilities. He had a hard time adjusting to Europe—and Europeans had a hard time adjusting to him.

Personal tensions between Bush and European leaders remained high over the next few months. During the German parliamentary elections, Chancellor Schroeder found himself in a tough election battle. Bush's plans for an invasion of Iraq were hugely unpopular in Germany, and when Schroeder opposed Bush's policy, his lead increased. The administration's anger grew when reporters wrote that Schroeder's justice minister had compared Bush with Hitler. The minister was alleged to have said that the United States "has a lousy legal system" and that "Bush would be sitting in prison today" for insider trading had current laws been on the books while he worked in the Texas oil industry. The minister rejected suggestions that Bush's war agenda against Iraq was over oil. A German newspaper quoted her as saying, "The Americans have enough oil." Rather, "Bush wants to distract attention from his domestic problems. This is a popular method. Hitler also used it." The minister later denied having uttered the words, and Schroeder refused to reappoint her to her post after the election. But the tensions had boiled over into a major crisis between longtime allies. The stress took months to ease.

The tensions between Bush and French president Chirac weighed heavily over the two-month-long Security Council debate over the resolution authorizing tough new weapons inspections in Iraq. In early November 2002, Chirac's government quietly suggested that it might circulate its own alternative to the American resolution, and its diplomats explored strategies for gathering support. The differences hung principally on issues of strategy—how strongly to push Hussein—not on issues of personality. But the frosty personal relationship between Bush and Chirac unquestionably complicated the already difficult job American diplomats faced in winning Security Council approval.

In November, in a unanimous vote, the Security Council finally approved the resolution. American negotiators convinced the French and Russians that the United States did not see the resolution as a license for invasion and that the country was committed to working with the UN to disarm Hussein. Bush's blunt, firm position in the end won the day. But the aw-shucks, fraternity-like informality that worked so well with so many Americans—Democrats and Republicans alike—served him poorly in Europe, straining several key relationships with key allies and undermining support for several key diplomatic initiatives.

2. IMPOSING RIGID DISCIPLINE THAT STIFLES DELIBERATION AND DEBATE

Team Bush demonstrated more discipline, focus, and efficiency in its first years than any presidential administration in recent memory. "If there is dissent within the administration, we never hear about it," one Washington reporter said. When the president makes a public appearance, he has a story to tell and steadfastly refuses to be distracted by other issues, regardless of the questions or agendas of the reporters covering the event.

Bush reviews his options crisply. He decides quickly. Aides tell of being intensely nervous before briefing the president. They knew they had only a minute or two to focus the issue, present the alternatives, and frame the options. It is not, they say, that the president is anti-intellectual. But he *is* very demanding. As a former White House official explained, "He is *very* focused on what is and is not 'presidential level.' He takes details—demands details—if he sees it at that level."

Bush is convinced that some predecessors—notably Carter and Clinton—allowed too many decisions about details to rise to the Oval Office. Carter aides proudly kept Carter's permission slips for the White House tennis courts as souvenirs, and few details were too small for Clinton to oversee. Like effective CEOs, Bush determined to focus his energy on only the top-level decisions. If a microissue did land on his desk, he forced aides to put the smaller pieces into the bigger picture. As a senior official noted, "He sniffs ill-conceived stuff by staff with almost unfailing intuition."

Other presidents—even his father—agonized far more when making decisions. Clinton and Gore both were famous for voraciously consuming briefing books the size of the Manhattan telephone directory. Bush demanded that his briefings be no longer than a couple of pages. He much prefers exploring details face-to-face.

The process has helped him focus on his agenda and stick religiously to his message. But the approach harbors big risks as well. It depends critically on his staffers' skill in boiling complex issues down to their essence. If they miss important facts, they risk blinding Bush to things he ought to know. It depends as well on Bush's instinct for sniffing out holes in the logic or gaps in the data. Aides report he is exceptionally good at it, but like any manager, he isn't perfect.

The process, then, risks making the president especially vulnerable to what he and his staff don't know—or don't know to ask. Complex problems are seldom easy to reduce to briefing books, let alone short memos. A staff as disciplined as Bush's can develop "groupthink" over time, and not know what they don't know. No matter how intense Bush's attention to a subject might be, his instincts for the jugular of some issues might not be as sharp as for others.

This Bush approach risks letting issues get away from the administration. As new, even more complex problems surface, all filled with vast uncertainties, the risks of not knowing what you don't know becomes magnified. "Reaching out and embracing different perspectives—it's not a strong enough part of the [administration's] approach," said one Washington insider who has worked with administration officials. "They do not reach out enough." To be sure, broader discussion rob the surprise factor and can take a lot of time. But as the insider noted, "You need to listen, decide, explain. You can get to a different place" and gain broader support by engaging in more debate and opening discussion to broader perspectives.

Missteps can escalate quickly, and unexpected problems can bubble up from unanticipated directions. Discipline and efficiency can sometimes wreak dangerous outcomes. With the unending avalanche of data and issues, it's a problem that all White Houses must inculcate themselves against.

For the Bush style, the risks are especially great. The problem came to the fore with the 2001 defection of Senator Jim Jeffords from the GOP. By focusing so much on getting his tax cut approved and building broader bipartisan support, Bush's team missed the risk that Jeffords's defection would pose. In another case, North Korea's nuclear saber rattling at the end of 2002 sought to take advantage of the administration while it was pinned down planning an attack on Iraq. A style of leadership determined to reduce everything to its black-and-white essence can pose serious risks in an increasingly gray world.

3. ALLOWING THE TEAM TO UNRAVEL

During its first two years in office, Team Bush showed remarkable cohesion—and remarkably little backbiting. The administration included some of Washington's most renowned and experienced in-fighters; yet, at least in public view, the policy debates were civil and the team remained tight.

Tight and disciplined, that is, except for the economic team. From almost the beginning, Bush's economic team attracted fierce fire. Unlike the foreign policy team—led by Rumsfeld, Powell, and Rice—the economic team seemed missing in action. As economic problems increased—the collapse of Enron, WorldCom, CEOs in handcuffs, a stock market crash, and a ballooning budget deficit—media attention on the economic policy team became intense. When team members fumbled several key decisions, public criticism, even among the president's friends, also grew.

Budget director Mitchell E. Daniels, Jr. took early shots for being abrasive with members of Congress. A former executive at Eli Lilly, Daniels came to Washington to be the tough guy in Bush's effort to hold the line on federal spending. That's why Bush nicknamed him "the Blade." Daniels took the moniker to heart in setting a tough position in dealing with Congress. In a widely read op-ed in the *Washington Post*, he roundly criticized budgetary practices in Congress. He wrote: "All the incomprehensible maneuvering and circumvention does more than waste time and, usually, taxpayer dollars; it demeans the practice of government and fuels public contempt for the entire process and the people accountable for it."

During the 2001 debate over Bush's tax cut plan, Daniels blasted Senate proposals to reduce the size of the cut. Disputes between budget directors and Congress are nothing unusual. The budget is often the flash point in the relationship between the White House and Capitol Hill, and the budget director is usually the point person in the conflict. But the senators trying to shrink the deficit were Republicans, and Daniels's harsh words not only caused conflict with Congress, they angered members of the president's own party. However, Bush continued to support Daniels with vigor—he was taking the strong line the administration needed on the budget.

The other members of the president's team encountered tougher criticism, though. Economic analysts complained that Treasury secretary Paul O'Neill's missteps spooked the markets. In the administration's first weeks, critics complained that O'Neill was talking down the economy and driving stock prices lower. When the market collapsed in 2002, critics argued that O'Neill should have taken a stronger role in rebuilding confidence.

O'Neill, a former CEO of Alcoa, prided himself as an executive who spoke his mind. As Treasury secretary, how-

ever, he was criticized for gaffes and inconsistency, for raising his voice but failing to inspire confidence. After
September 11, he urged investors to buy stocks and predicted a big upswing in prices (stocks dropped precipitous-
ly). A February 2002 statement in Germany saying that the
U.S. was not pursuing a strong dollar policy caused the dollar's value to fall sharply and led to a quick clarification by
Treasury officials in Washington.

In June 2002 he said that "throwing the U.S. taxpayers'
money" at Brazil "doesn't seem brilliant to me," a statement
that drove down prices on the Brazilian financial markets
and provoked Brazilian president Fernando Henrique
Cardoso to call Condoleezza Rice to complain. When stock
prices were falling in June, O'Neill was touring Africa with
Irish rock singer Bono. One investment manager in New
York complained, "He doesn't inspire much confidence." In
fact, "He seems to put his foot in his mouth and stumble. I
don't think he's helping the cause." One Republican business
leader was far more brusque, saying: "There are a lot of people who would like to see him gone in the next half hour."

The chairman of the National Economic Council,
Lawrence B. Lindsey, was disparaged for being disorgan-
ized. Lindsey came regularly to Austin during the 2000
campaign to tutor Bush on economic issues, and he was a
prime architect of the $1.3 billion tax cut. As a scholar in
the capital's American Enterprise Institute, Lindsey was a
Washington insider. Within the administration, however,
Republican insiders questioned whether he had the political
skills for the job. After the 2002 midterm elections, Bush
decided O'Neill and Lindsey had to go. He sent Vice
President Cheney to deliver the news, and both officials
resigned the next day.

The administration's biggest problem, however, came in securities regulation. Harvey L. Pitt was widely regarded as one of the nation's best lawyers. He had previously served in the Securities and Exchange Commission, and he seemed an ideal appointment to head the SEC in the Bush administration. The Senate confirmed him unanimously. But his troubles began almost immediately, and in just 14 months he became a "political piñata," as one Democrat in Congress labeled him.

Aides complained he was mercurial, sometimes brilliant, sometimes obsessing over insignificant details. Observers criticized him for too often relying on old friends instead of the SEC's experienced career staff. He obsessed over secrecy. Senior commission officials came to believe they could not trust him. In addition, Pitt rankled members of Congress by suggesting his position ought to be elevated to cabinet status, a change that would have brought him increased prestige and a higher salary.

Amid the personal turmoil, Pitt received deafening criticism for failing to get ahead of the collapse of Enron and WorldCom. He signaled he was about to appoint John H. Biggs, chairman of TIAA-CREF (the huge firm that manages pensions for college teachers), to head the new board to oversee the accounting industry. Biggs was well-known for his tough views and for his commitment to frame stricter rules for accountants. Several weeks later, however, he surprised both Biggs and many observers by instead appointing William H. Webster, former director of both the CIA and the FBI.

Just a few days after the SEC approved Webster for the post, however, Webster revealed he had headed the audit committee of U.S. Technologies, a company later accused of fraud. For the new top cop of the accounting industry, the revelation was poison. Pitt and Webster soon resigned, Pitt on election night in 2002. "The auditing of the auditors has been as reliable as the auditors themselves," the *Washington Post* wrote in a critical editorial.

Bush quickly put together a new economic team. CSX executive John Snow became Treasury secretary, and Stephen Friedman, former chairman of Goldman Sachs, took over as head of the National Economic Council. Aetna executive and investment analyst William H. Donaldson was named to chair the Securities and Exchange Commission. Snow and Donaldson had both served in the Ford administration—Snow in the Transportation Department, Donaldson in the State Department.

Like Bush's other key appointments, they shared ties to Bush and his family. Donaldson had met Bush's uncle at Yale and was an old friend of his father. Snow had participated with Bush in a roundtable discussion on the economy. Friedman had served on Bush's foreign intelligence advisory board.

With the appointments, Bush sought two things. First, he wanted to name smart, strong, commanding figures whose presence could help calm the financial markets and convey *gravitas*, a term discussed much but seldom used to describe Bush's first economic team. Second, he wanted powerful team members who supported the administration's economic strategy and vigorously conveyed the message. In naming Snow, for example, he said that the new secretary would be "a key advocate of my administration's agenda for growth, new jobs, and wider, more international trade."

Bush's problems with his first economic team were surprising and tinged with irony. After all, he was an MBA with a deep business background. He built his team with business executives, and the officials he named to the key economic posts were all trusted, experienced advisers. But some of his appointees, like Pitt and O'Neill, never fared well in the Washington fishbowl. The first economic team proved unable to effectively articulate the administration's policies. Discipline alone wasn't enough, and Bush hoped for better with his second team.

4. MAKING BLACK-AND-WHITE DECISIONS IN A SHADES-OF-GRAY WORLD

Especially after the September 11 terrorist attacks, Bush stirred widespread approval for his strong stand and pledge to avenge the thousands of lives lost. He told Americans he wanted to bring Osama bin Laden to justice "dead or alive." He called the terrorists "evildoers" and "barbaric people." He called for allies to stand "with us or against us." A month after the attacks, he told Americans that al Qaeda was "on the run." And in a pointed jab at Bill Clinton, who once tried to take out bin Laden with a cruise missile attack but hit only empty tents and sand, Bush was blunt, saying:

When I take action, I'm not going to fire a $2 million missile at a ten dollar empty tent and hit a camel in the butt.

That style framed a sharp, decisive response to the terrorist attacks. But that approach did not work well when applied to other thornier issues, for which black-white, "with us or against us" responses were not appropriate. For example, just a few months after the attacks, the Middle East erupted in a new series of Palestinian bombings of

Israeli buses and Israeli retaliations against Palestinian strongholds. It was a problem with no real answer.

As was the case for virtually every president since World War II, Bush found himself drawn into the Middle East fray. More than most presidents, he had tried to skirt the controversy, for he and his advisers saw it as a no-win swamp. And just as his predecessors failed to settle the issue, a stable solution for the ageless problem eluded Bush as well. A president can scarcely be criticized for failing to find a way out of the swamp. It's been a seething problem for decades, predating even the creation of the state of Israel.

However, the case raises a deeper issue about the Bush style and how it can fail when confronting complex problems. In dealing with these puzzling issues, his instinct was to ground them in his deeply felt values. The ultimate question is whether new problems might, at some point, push into territory that his value system did not chart, and whether he—and his team—might become blind to subtle and unexpected implications.

5. LOSING CONTROL OF THE AGENDA

Bush's style comes from the MBA playbook: focus on the big issues, decide on the major strategy questions, and delegate the details. He's practiced it more than any president ever has. The style, in turn, has framed the way the rest of the White House staff has worked. Bush created both the aura and the reality of command, built around a strong team.

With that style, however, comes the risk that the top leader can appear disconnected. The president built a team composed of strong people, both as aides and cabinet secretaries. Strong people don't like to be told what to do. When a leader allows his strong-willed team members to set the agenda and handle the details, there's a possibility that people will perceive that leader as being isolated from the real action. A top leader's effort to decide and delegate can appear detached and toothless.

During the summer of 2002, in fact, the roiling debate over the administration's Iraq policy spilled over onto the front pages of the nation's leading newspapers. Colin Powell's concerns about building a diplomatic base and a broader coalition for military action found their way into print. Plans for military strategy—suggesting a quick, surgical campaign and prolonged, house-to-house urban warfare—played out in the media. The debate appeared endless, spilling from weeks into months. Observers wondered why the battle was so prolonged, whether Bush was overwhelmed by the details, whether he truly was master of his staff or whether the staff was in fact mastering him.

His forceful UN speech on September 12 put the speculation to rest. Bush clearly was in charge of policy. But for the first time in the two years of the Bush administration, the protracted debate raised serious speculation about who was in charge. At the least, the turmoil created a problem of appearance. At the most, it established the possibility that the appearance might, under the right circumstances, turn into reality: that the staff would become master of the house instead.

6. DRIVING AWAY THOSE WHO DON'T SHARE YOUR VISION

Team Bush, if nothing else, quickly became the most tightly managed White House operation in recent memory. Internal dissent in the Carter and Reagan administrations regularly appeared in newspaper headlines, with warring leaks captivating Washington insiders. Those leaks, and the scuttlebutt they produced, undermined the Carter administration (even before it got started) and weakened the Reagan juggernaut.

Some of those battles spilled over into the first Bush administration. Bush 43 watched some of the disputes first-hand and helped resolve some of them as his father's enforcer. His own resolve was that his administration would not suffer a plague of leaks and disloyalty. Some of his team members were champion "leakers" in the old days, but Bush clearly communicated an unmistakable message. They were part of *his* team. Once the president made a decision, he expected them to follow loyally, without public brawls or private backstabbing.

The administration did indeed show remarkable cohesion on even the most difficult issues. During the summer of 2002, the public debate among his aides about what to do about Iraq—and how to do it—threatened to unravel the administration's loyalty and discipline. But the vigorous struggle, with stories planted in the newspapers by opposing camps, stopped immediately when Bush announced his policy before the United Nations. The remarkable fact was the dog that didn't bark. Unlike most big decisions in previous administrations, there was none of the second-guessing, media tales of internal struggle and controversy, or deep background stories of continued debate. The internal debates occurred. The president decided. And his team fell in line.

The administration was not able to exact the same loyalty from those outside the inner circle. That was especially the case with Republican members of Congress, who enjoyed their own political base and didn't always see eye-to-eye with the president's strategy. The loss of Senator

Jeffords from the Republican party showed how difficult managing these outside players could be—and the large risk that missteps could cause. The challenge of building loyalty among members of this larger team grew exponentially the further out the team was from Bush's inner circle. Similarly, the president's tools for leveraging the team diminished. Those problems sometimes frustrated Bush.

In dealing with these problems, Bush 41's style had been very different from Bush 43's. Bush senior had served in both the House and Senate, and as president, he paid a great deal of attention to members of Congress. He'd spent years building relationships he would later rely on as president. He often made phone calls from the Oval Office to touch base with key members. He exercised in the House gym and often invited old pals to Camp David. And when his aides threatened to use hardball tactics to round up key votes, Bush 41 instructed his staff to back off.

In contrast, Bush 43 had no Capitol Hill experience and didn't have personal relationships with members of Congress when he came to Washington. When Jeffords opposed the president's tax cut plan, Bush did not call him to try to change his mind. He allowed his staff free rein in playing hardball behind the scenes. Some observers did not find that surprising—after all, Bush himself had sometimes played the role of enforcer in Bush 41's administration.

Team Bush learned a critical lesson too late. To win, it's important to win votes in Congress. That requires maintaining a solid and committed base of true believers. It requires being attentive to moderate swing votes (like Jeffords) and massaging them with the vast resources of perks and power at the White House's disposal. It was a mistake that Team Bush did not make twice. In fact, Bush took a huge gamble in investing his personal prestige in helping Republican candidates in the 2002 midterm congressional campaign. The gamble paid off richly. Team Bush then worked to parlay that into legislative success—and a jump-start for the 2004 presidential campaign.

7. LOSING SUPPORT OF IMPORTANT OUTSIDE CONSTITUENCIES

Along with the Team Bush penchant for disciplined pursuit of strategy and message came a proclivity for closed-door, closed-mouth decisions. Leaks were rare and leakers quickly found themselves on the outside looking in. There simply wasn't a presidency in memory that managed such tight control of the decision-making process.

The secrecy of the administration's discussions, however, sometimes caused serious problems. Amid the turmoil of the California energy crisis, Bush asked Vice President Cheney to convene a national energy policy development group. It included high-ranking members of the administration, but it met as well with several executives of major energy businesses. Reporters got wind of the group's conversations with the energy executives and asked the White House to reveal the names of those senior managers.

After the White House refused, environmental groups filed suit. Some members of Congress asked the congressional investigative organization, the General Accounting Office, to investigate. All of them were suspicious of the plan, which urged the expansion of oil exploration and drilling and the opening of the Arctic National Wildlife Refuge for energy development. They worried that the group had closeted itself in secret, listened mainly to pro-oil officials, ignored pro-conservation groups, and crafted a policy that would spoil the environment.

A federal judge, Gladys Kessler of the U.S. District Court in Washington, ordered the administration to produce some of the group's documents. She wondered "what in the world" the Energy Department was doing in delaying a response to Freedom of Information Act requests. In her order, Kessler wrote, "The government can offer no legal or practical excuse for its excessive delay."

When the administration refused the GAO's request, the dispute eventually developed into a high-stakes lawsuit. For the first time in its history, the GAO filed suit against a federal official. The GAO wanted the court to order Cheney to turn over records about who the group met with, how much it spent, and where the money came from. GAO attorneys pointed to legislation that gave it the right to audit the expenditure of federal funds.

Cheney's lawyers countered that GAO was acting beyond its authority. "They seek to compel the vice president to give up documents that would show his and his closest advisers' decision-making," said the principal deputy solicitor, General Paul Clement. "This is unprecedented. It would allow a revolution in the separation of powers." The "revolutionary" language was no empty rhetoric. The stakes were huge: for energy policy, for the way the Bush administration did its business, and for the balance of power between Congress and the White House. In December 2002 a federal judge ruled that the GAO did not have standing in court to challenge Cheney, but the battle underlined the struggle that Bush's strategy would inevitably court.

When Bush proposed the creation of a Department of Homeland Security in June 2002, it was a plan developed in greater secrecy—secret even from members of his team. It was a sweeping proposal: perhaps the greatest single reorganization in American history, bringing together more than 20 federal agencies and almost 170,000 employees, and crossing the jurisdiction of 88 different congressional committees and subcommittees.

Chief of Staff Card had led a small team that worked in secret to develop the plan. Many of the cabinet officials who would lose agencies to the new department found out about the plan only the day before the president's speech. The speech itself was timed to derail growing congressional demands for stronger federal action. It also distracted attention from Colleen Rowley's testimony before Congress. She was the agent in the FBI Minneapolis field office who had written a blistering memo to the bureau's headquarters charging that pre-September 11 warnings about suspicious characters seeking flight training had been ignored.

Just as congressional attention to her memo was picking up steam, Bush's announcement of the proposal knocked the story out of the newspapers. It was a true masterwork of strategy and timing. After having fought the creation of the new department since the attacks, the administration was losing ground quickly in the debate. The president's proposal shifted the debate from whether—to how—the new department should be created, helping Bush regain the upper hand. His own team members were shocked to discover that they had lost agencies, budgets, and personnel—the coins of the realm in capital power circles. The quick announcement helped blunt the congressional attack, but it stirred up endless, pained questions from those affected.

Those questions about the "who" and the "how" contributed to the five-month delay in passing the bill. In the end, the Republican victories at the midterm elections helped Team Bush get more of what it wanted from Congress than might have been the case had Congress acted earlier. But the battle spelled out a warning of the debate-in-secret, decide-in-a-flash style that characterized many of the administration's important decisions. In developing decisions among only a small circle of advisers, the administration not only risks being blindsided by unanticipated issues (see Trap 2 above). It also risks undermining its ability to gel support around the decisions it makes.

BUSH LESSONS

1. **Don't try the same touch with everyone.** Find the approach that works best for each key player.

2. **To avoid groupthink, stimulate internal discussion and debate.** Not knowing what you don't think to ask can sometimes pose the biggest risks.

3. **Loyal, experienced team members aren't enough.** Matching their skills and style to the job to be done is just as important as it is for the leader.

4. **Being decisive is critical, but sharp decisions don't fit every problem.** Good leaders know how to balance hard and soft approaches to achieve success.

5. **Internal debate is healthy and essential.** It can even help distance the leader from the fallout of tough decisions. But never let anyone forget who makes—and owns—the big decisions.

6. Make room on the team for those who, at first blush, may not seem to fit. They could become critical allies— or dangerous enemies.

7. Maintain discipline on message and strategy—but don't sacrifice the chance to broaden support for the plan.

Winning the
Expectations Game

*"I've got confidence in my capabilities.
I love to be underestimated."*

—GEORGE W. BUSH, QUOTED IN U.S.A. TODAY, JUNE 8, 2000

*"What we anticipate seldom occurs;
what we least expected generally happens."*

—BENJAMIN DISRAELI

PERHAPS THE MOST consistent thing about George W. Bush's career is that he has consistently exceeded expectations. Texas punsters said he wasn't a bush but a "shrub," and the joke fueled a best-seller by columnist Molly Ivins. But the joke ultimately was on those who underestimated him.

The profits from his oil business paid for his ownership share of the Texas Rangers. When he sold that share, he realized a $15 million return. Few analysts gave him a chance of unseating Texas governor Ann Richards in 1994, yet he beat her in the race. Political handicappers gave him slim odds for a successful gubernatorial term, but he rolled to a huge victory in 1998. He explored a presidential run, but cynics suggested he wasn't nearly smart enough to be the nation's chief executive. When he won the nomination, Democrats relished the idea of Al Gore taking him on in the debates, but he astounded everyone by holding his own.

He won the prolonged presidential race but many doubted his chances of accomplishing anything meaningful. A December 2000 *USA Today*/CNN poll revealed that people did not believe that Bush and congressional Democrats could put politics aside to work together. Only a little more than one in three voters believed it would be possible.

With the September 11 terrorist attacks, Bush faced the biggest foreign policy challenge in a generation and emerged with unprecedented approval ratings. Critics predicted that he would stumble or that the postattack public opinion high would evaporate, but he ended his first two years in office with approval ratings in impressive territory.

PLAYING THE EXPECTATIONS GAME

Bush has always been easy to underestimate. He was a C student at Yale better known for partying than studying. His first political race, a run for Congress, ended in defeat. His penchant for malapropisms became well known, with Web sites devoted to cataloguing his misuse of words. Crispin Miller's *The Bush Dyslexicon* is a treasure trove of Bush favorites, and NBC's *Saturday Night Live* celebrated his "strategery." Bush himself made fun of his own fractured syntax in the 2002 HBO documentary *Journeys with George*.

Bush has made playing the expectations game into an art form. He started with expectations very low indeed. One Republican pollster, Whit Ayres, was pleased with that. "It makes it all the easier for President Bush to succeed," he said in January 2001. Democrats realized the trap. Senate Democratic leader Tom Daschle worried, "I think we underestimate this man at our own peril."

The cycle of underestimating Bush only to have him exceed expectations ought to be a cliché by now, but he continues to surprise his critics and amaze his friends. Bush understands that one of his greatest strengths is that his public, easygoing, frat-boy style encourages people to underestimate his leadership. Most people don't see him as a focused behind-the-scenes, hard-driving, decision-oriented executive. Leadership always revolves around expectations. Success depends on beating them.

In fact, Bush's core strategy has been to encourage low expectations and then exceed them. Especially in his first weeks in office, he constantly reminded everyone that expectations were low, and he repeated his determination that his administration succeed. During a discussion about his tax cut program at a March 2001 press conference, he said: "Those who think that they can say we're only going to have a stimulus package, but let's forget tax relief, mis-underestimate—excuse me, underestimate ... [laughter] ... just making sure you were paying attention. [Laughter.] You were. [Laughter.] Underestimate our administration's resolve to get this done. Bush repeated the phrase "low expectations" scores of times in his first two years in office, and especially during the first weeks. It was a call to action for his allies and a challenge to his opponents.

This central element of Bush's style continued to work over and over again. It was all the more remarkable because, like a batter facing a pitcher with the bases loaded, everyone knew that a fastball was coming. The strategy is battle-tested and keeps working.

BUILD CAPITAL TO SPEND IT

Effective leadership depends on the political capital leaders have to spend. Some leaders start with a large supply; some with little. Leaders can only act if they have the capital to reinforce their decisions. Fighting battles drains capital. Winning them can help build it. John F. Kennedy's defense secretary, Robert McNamara, charted it on a graph: "You come into office at zero years, and you've got eight years ahead of you, hopefully." The key, he told Kennedy, was lasting the eight years, accomplishing as much as possible, and spending all the political capital as he walked out the door. It's impossible to act effectively without political capital; political capital unused is opportunity forgone.

Bush held that as a central principle of leadership. He watched his father's painful lesson. With his Gulf War triumph, Bush 41's approval rating soared to 91 percent. He looked virtually unbeatable, with the presidential election just a year away. But he did not put his political capital to work. It slowly eroded, and by November 2002, Bill Clinton handily defeated him.

From his father's experience, Bush drew an important conclusion: Capital is useful only to the degree it can help build more support—it must be used or it will be lost. Pressed by *USA Today*'s Walter Shapiro to talk about his father's failed presidential reelection campaign, he explained: "My dad had earned enormous capital from the Gulf War, and . . .

> *the proper application of political capital is very important. You have to earn it, but you also have to spend it, because capital atrophies if it's not spent."*

In a typically Bush case of underlining his message by repeating it constantly, he told the *Wall Street Journal*'s editorial board the same thing in almost precisely the same words. The importance of building capital, investing it, and gaining a larger return to support even more decisions is a central tenet of his style.

Chief executives do not start with a large stock of capital. If they're lucky, the process that selected them provides a small starter supply, but their first steps can quickly erode that away. Clinton's decision to advance recognition of gays in the military, for example, began undermining his support within his first weeks as president. But if earning capital is hard, not using the capital at hand is worse. If it's not spent, it dwindles, and there's no central bank from which to borrow more. Only by investing and spending capital can it grow.

Bush saw what happened when his father failed to invest and spend. He believed that Clinton dissipated his capital into too many areas—he wanted to be both the environmental president and the education president. Bush's instincts had long been to focus sharply but carefully on a narrow agenda on which he could produce victories—and then use those victories to build support for bigger issues.

In his first race for governor, he hammered away on his four basic themes: juvenile justice reform, tort reform, welfare reform, and education reform. When he became governor, as one reporter explained, "It was as if everyone had underestimated him and by the time they wised up he was in control." He championed each of those issues and built a successful, ambitious legislative agenda in a state where the governor starts with little political capital.

In Bush's 1998 reelection bid, "he and Rove went for broke," *Washington Post* columnist David S. Broder wrote. He bombarded potential supporters by mail and phone. He not only won reelection by a margin of two to one, but also brought the lieutenant governor, attorney general, and comptroller positions from Democratic hands into the Republican camp. And, of course, he rode his reelection success to the presidency.

All the while, people continued to underestimate him. Comedians poked fun at his mangled syntax—and he often joined in. After his election, Molly Ivins couldn't resist writing, "O.K., he's not the brightest porch light on the block." Of course, he never claimed to be.

He was only an average student, and he struggled during the 2000 campaign to master the intricacies of diplomacy. He overcame his limitations by building a strong staff, especially in foreign policy—people who knew more than he did about each of their subjects. But he worked hard to build them into a coherent team and he never let them forget who was boss. If he wasn't the brightest porch light on the block, he proved he was bright enough to be elected president of the United States.

Bush was the living embodiment of Peter F. Drucker's dictum: "To be effective is the job of the executive." Drucker argues that "there seems to be little correlation between a man's effectiveness and his intelligence." In fact, "Brilliant men are often strikingly ineffectual; they fail to realize that brilliant insight is not by itself achievement."

Bush defined success as being effective. And being effective was defining his agenda and putting it into place. He nurtured his capital to get the job done—and in doing the job, he saw his capital increase. In mid-year 2002, his public support was high. With the 2002 midterm election approaching, and with considerable domestic concern about a possible war with Iraq, Democrats were nipping at his heels. He had the choice of carefully husbanding his capital—or investing it heavily. He had seen what happened to his father's huge reservoir, and he determined he would not follow the same path. For Bush 43, the choice was to spend the capital to create even more of it.

BUILD NARROW SUPPORT INTO A BROAD BASE

As the 2002 midterm elections approached, Karl Rove developed a strategy for a full-court press. Conventional wisdom is that the party of incumbent presidents always loses seats in Congress in the midterm elections. That has held true for every midterm election in the last century, except for Democratic party wins in 1934 on the coattails of Roosevelt's enormous popularity. Most policy issues don't matter. The real question is how many seats the party will lose. On average, Republican strategist Mary Matalin estimated, the party loses 30 House seats and two in the Senate. But Rove believed that the strategic application of presidential presence and power could reverse the trajectory of history. Bush decided to put a good many of his chips on Rove's poker table, and Air Force One hopped around the country to stump for Republican candidates.

In Arizona, Matt Salmon, Republican candidate for governor, ached for a photo of him and the president emerging triumphantly from the front door of the presidential airplane. He drove two and a half hours to Flagstaff so he could fly back to Phoenix with the president. "I would have crawled on broken glass" for the picture, Salmon said. And he got it. Candidates for House seats rode along.

Taking to the road for Republican candidates was a huge gamble. Presidents risk draining their own political capital if the candidates they campaign for stumble. Democrats often complained that Bill Clinton did not work nearly hard enough to help his party's congressional candidates. But Clinton team knew he faced tough struggles ahead and needed to husband his power.

For Bush, the 2002 strategy paid off handsomely. His party not only broke the 1934 record, but Bush became the first Republican since Theodore Roosevelt to gain seats in both houses during a midterm election. In fact, the party's success spilled over into state legislatures. Republicans gained 200 seats around the country; on average, the president's party tends to lose 350 seats.

"Bush was critical," said North Carolina Republican chairman Bill Cobey. "Without his help we couldn't have raised the kind of money we had for getting out the vote." The get-out-the-vote campaign helped push Elizabeth Dole to victory over Erskine Bowles, former chief of staff for Bill Clinton. In state after state, Bush's frenetic last-minute campaigning helped Republicans eke out close wins.

The strategy was one that Bush had mastered in Texas. As David Broder explained, Bush "started with a narrow win in his first race for governor and, step by step, converted it into a broader and more lasting victory for the Republican party." It was a strategy he brought with him to the White House, as he built his razor-thin electoral college victory—and overcame his loss in the popular vote—to win passage of his income tax cut. Bush repeatedly surprised his political foes by pursuing policies they thought he was too weak to win, and then by winning victories that seemed beyond his reach.

The congressional wins were extremely narrow—just a small number of votes in a handful of races. Some Democrats were not convinced that the win was a mandate. "It was a 50-50 country before the election, and it's still a 50-50 country," argued the Democratic Leadership Council's Al From. "I don't think this is an overwhelming mandate." But press secretary Ari Fleischer turned on the message machine full-blast. "It is a big victory," he asserted to reporters. Even Tony Coehlo, chairman of Al Gore's 2000 presidential campaign, agreed. "The White House took a huge gamble; they rolled the dice, and it worked," he said. In fact, Coehlo concluded, "They won the 2000 election legitimately last night. He got his mandate, he got his victory and now he can govern for two years."

Through a handful of victories by narrow margins, Team Bush gambled and won. "He moves boldly even when he doesn't have any political capital," explained longtime capital observer Thomas Mann, of Washington's Brookings Institution. "He moves to create capital." By investing that capital, Bush won a significant victory, and his communications team then worked hard to interpret that victory into a mandate. A senior White House official contended that Bush "thinks the conventional wisdom about how you respond to a big victory is wrong." Instead of retreating to complacency, the official said, "it strengthens your hand" to act.

USE THE BROAD BASE TO CHAMPION POLICY

Bush aimed to translate his electoral success into a two-pronged policy strategy. First, on the international front, he carried over popular support for his war on terrorism into a campaign to disarm Iraq's Saddam Hussein. Second, on the domestic front, he worked to cement his first-year tax cut into an enduring economic stimulus plan. Together, the two elements would become the strategy for his reelection bid, a combination of policy decisions and political tactics that he believed would secure his reelection and his legacy.

EXAMPLE: THE BUSH DOCTRINE

Bush and his advisers denied that he was driven by the failure of his father to win reelection, but the parallels were too obvious to ignore. In the Gulf War, Bush 41 halted American troops short of a campaign to remove Hussein. At the time, his advisers believed that continuing the war would risk splintering the multinational coalition, and that, in turn, would turn the effort from success to failure. The result was that Hussein remained in power.

George W. Bush and his advisers argued that the Iraqi dictator was building stockpiles of dangerous weapons and that he might very well use them, either directly or by supplying terrorists. They worried in particular that Hussein might acquire a nuclear weapon. Stopping him before he became more fully armed—and even more dangerous—became the administration's foremost national security goal.

The first part of Bush's international plan was a huge gamble. It framed a new strategy, christened the "Bush doctrine," that sought to chart a new role for America in the world. In a speech at West Point, Bush said: "We fight, as we always fight, for a just peace—a peace that favors liberty. We will defend the peace against the threats from terrorists and tyrants. We will preserve the peace by building good relations among the great powers. And we will extend the peace by encouraging free and open societies on every continent." It built on the argument that communism had fallen, that the Cold War was over, and that the United States was the world's lone remaining superpower. "America is now threatened less by conquering states than we are by failing ones," the president's national security strategy concluded. Bush expanded the old notion of imminent threat—that a nation was justified in launching an attack when opposing armies mobilized and threatened war. He crafted it into a new strategy of "preemptive attack." If the United States sensed that the risks of a terrorist attack were rising, the nation would act preemptively to prevent it. It was better, the Bush doctrine suggested, to act first against the new breed of concealed surprise attacks than to risk the mass casualties and catastrophic damage of an attack such as the one that occurred on September 11.

In line with this doctrine, Bush and his foreign policy team believed that Iraq had an arsenal of weapons of mass destruction that could harm the United States and its allies, and that the weapons might find their way into terrorist hands. Better to force Iraq to disarm, this line of thinking went, than to risk the potential catastrophe that such weapons might deliver. And better to go to war with Iraq if Iraq refused to disarm.

Foreign policy experts agreed that an Iraq armed with weapons of mass destruction would be intolerably dangerous. But they disagreed on what weapons Hussein had, when he might develop more, and thus how dangerous he might be. They also disagreed strongly on the "with us or against us," go-it-alone strategy that underlay the Bush doctrine. But the Bush administration was determined to press ahead.

Perhaps the most notable thing about the decision was the subtle yet crucial shift in strategy. Bush's foreign policy advisers had identified Iraq as a major threat long before September 11. They had long planned an initiative to disarm Hussein. But then September 11 intervened. Their attention immediately shifted to the war against terrorism, which had widespread political support. With the Bush doctrine, Team Bush sought to shift the focus from terrorists to states that might support terrorists—and, among those states, to Iraq in particular. Team Bush also sought to parlay public support for the war against Osama bin Laden to a campaign against Saddam Hussein. It was a textbook case of the Bush strategy: building capital to use capital.

EXAMPLE: ECONOMIC STRATEGY

Bush was also keenly aware that his father had failed to capitalize on the success of the Gulf War and on the huge surge of public support that accompanied it. The economy weakened in the months following that war, and it dragged down Bush 41's hopes for a second term. In Bush 43's case, as the economy limped through 2002, its sluggishness was seen as a major threat, in both policy and political terms. And Bush and Rove were determined not to repeat the fate of Bush 41. So it came as no surprise that Bush dumped his economic team soon after the midterm congressional elections and installed a new team.

The job of these new economic appointments was to trumpet the message of economic growth. The Bush Team believes strongly in the power of positive rhetoric for shoring up the economy—that confidence will help spur investment and stimulate spending. In addition, the new appointments were to help frame and sell the stimulus plan Bush assembled for early 2003.

Bush faced enormous pressure from his conservative flank to impose quick tax cuts to spur economic growth. Supply siders believed that Ronald Reagan's tax cuts had helped spur the economy during the 1980s, and that by draining tax revenue from the system, he had curbed the growth of government spending. These supply siders wanted big and immediate tax cuts. In contrast, moderates were convinced that the projections of large deficits that would balloon in the future demanded a retreat from tax cuts toward a balanced budget.

Bush took a surprising middle ground. The 2001 tax cuts were temporary, scheduled to expire in 10 years. He argued that the cuts ought to be made permanent. It was a long-term strategy that looked past the short-term demands of the supply siders and the budget-balancing fears of the moderates. The president pushed permanent repeal of the estate tax, a longtime favorite of conservatives. He remained ready to pump more money into the economy if it showed further sluggishness—and to adopt (and take credit for) Democratic ideas if the tactics suggested it was the right move. In 2002, the polls gave Bush more credit for steering the economy than the Democrats, and he was determined to keep it that way.

PLUCK AND LUCK: A WINNING COMBINATION

Bush has long concentrated sharply on decision-making as the focus of his style and behavior. He strongly believes that the most important thing he can do is to decide, and thereby chart the course for his team—and the nation—to follow. He's tough and he sticks to his guns. "He's made a science out of selling tough partisan proposals with cool rhetoric," the Brookings Institution's Thomas Mann argues.

Having little political capital never slowed him down. He seized on even weak positions as chances to create capital and, once it was created, to broaden his base and deepen his support. Not only does he not shy away from risks—he sees them as opportunities. He has kept to a short, sharp agenda, and insists on absolute discipline among his team members in pursuing it.

As decision maker, Bush has placed great confidence in his own compass. He believes he knows what is right, and he's determined to follow that course. However, as new and unanticipated problems arise, he's shown himself to be remarkably adaptable. He's open to persuasion by his staff about *how* to pursue any given course of action—but he is a leader who insists on great loyalty when he decides *what* should be done.

In the debate over war with Iraq, for example, Bush asserted that Hussein had weapons of mass destruction and committed his administration to removing Hussein. Some aides argued forcefully that the United States should not wait for other nations to fall in line. Others argued that a go-it-alone approach would not be accepted either by the American people or by important allies. Bush ultimately decided to work with the United Nations in an approach based upon coalition-building. But he did not retreat from his basic conviction that Hussein had weapons that had to go, and he moved the debate from *whether* to remove those weapons to *how* best to do so.

Some analysts have argued that Bush, like the nation, was fundamentally changed by September 11. The reality is that Bush, in the aftermath of September 11, was essentially the same as the president sworn in on January 20, 2001—and the man who served as Texas governor. New problems created a far more complex political chessboard on the geopolitical front. But the man and his style remained fundamentally the same, deeply grounded in an MBA approach to decision-making and leadership.

There's one final, essential point about the Bush style worth noting: He had a long run of incredible luck. "So much of politics and public life is chance and serendipity," Mann concludes. That is true in spades of George W. Bush. He won the presidency in the courts even though it was likely that thousands of Florida voters who intended to vote for Al Gore voted for Pat Buchanan by mistake. He pushed through his tax cut as a matter of principle, but budget deficits began rising soon afterward. He struggled to get the next stage of his agenda moving, but September 11 intervened with unprecedented challenges—and opportunities—for leadership. His party won the 2002 midterm congressional elections, but only by a few votes in a few congressional districts.

While luck has played a role in the Bush victories, it is obviously not luck alone that has determined his fate. Bush has demonstrated an uncommon knack for cobbling together winning positions from the narrowest of bases. He's broadened his support by pulling together surprising coalitions. He's shown a keen judgment for choosing the issues most likely to help him do just that, and for adapting the issues in the heat of battle. Thus, he has certainly helped make his own luck. But he has unquestionably benefited from circumstances that, in turn, provided him with enormous opportunities.

BUSH LESSONS

These principles frame the core of Bush's style:

- Decide firmly from principle.

- Shape tactics pragmatically.

- Insist on loyalty from team members in pursuing those tactics.

- Devise a clear message and then sell the plan.

- Use success to broaden the base, enhance the chances for further success—and exceed expectations.

The Strength of
a Leader

*" ... the executive is, first of all,
expected to get the right things done."*

PETER DRUCKER

BY ANY STANDARD, George W. Bush has been a remarkably effective executive. Not only is he the nation's first MBA president, he is also, to borrow from Gilbert and Sullivan, the very model of a modern MBA executive. For Bush, the *decision* is the central presidential act.

Bush's decisions build on the hard work of his team members. He counts on them to identify the issues, probe the facts, develop the options, and explore the implications. In the end, though, there can be no mistaking who is running the show, with an uncommon focus and discipline.

However, though Bush's style has proven effective, it would be dangerous to suggest that *all* managers—or all presidents—ought to pursue such a style. What is most important about the Bush style is that *it works for him*. The lesson is not that managers ought to copy the successful style of another leader. Rather, the lesson is the broader strategy: Find a style that works, that produces results, and then stick religiously to it.

But being effective—getting things done—isn't the only measure of an executive. As Drucker reminds us, the key is not only getting things done, but it's also *getting the right things done*—and *getting things done right*. Weak decisions produce weak results. Strong decisions can produce strong results. But wrong decisions, even if well-executed, can push the executive—and the nation—off course.

A major risk of the Team Bush style is using old templates for new, complex, and fast-changing issues. Bush is one of the most grounded presidents the nation has seen in our lifetimes. He decides by sifting problems and options through his fundamental values. But if his decisions are black and white, the problems facing him are gray. Relying on deep values can bring uncommon discipline and focus. But it can also blind the leader to deceptively subtle new problems that don't fit old strategies. Balancing the need for focus and consistent strategy with a shrewd eye for new puzzles is an especially important problem for the Bush style.

Another major risk of the Team Bush style is overreaching. Convinced of the rightness of the cause and relying on great skill in building support, Team Bush can easily overestimate its political strength and the public's support for its initiatives. As in the 2002 midterm congressional elections, Bush has sometimes been a high-stakes gambler. A miscalculated gamble could leave him exposed, in both policy and political terms. His style is built on the premise that political capital that isn't invested will be lost. But political capital placed on risky bets could drain his capital to zero and weaken his presidency, suddenly and dramatically.

The Team Bush style, more than most, courts serious dangers. It can be a special problem for teams that become too sheltered from outside ideas, new information, and different perspectives—and for teams so confident in their ability that they outrun their support.

Of course, *all* styles carry risks. Richard Nixon's obsession with control ultimately cost him his presidency. Jimmy Carter's impulse for the common touch seemed to diminish him and make him seem less presidential. Ronald Reagan's penchant for delegation led to a loss of control over Central American policy. And Bush 41's focus on international issues blinded him to the risks of a sluggish domestic economy.

Bush 43 is certainly not oblivious to the risks his style poses. However, he is also keenly sensitive to the possibility that worrying too much about the risks could undermine his ability to act. He clearly believes that there is a strong purpose for his presidency. Not to pursue it, strongly and aggressively, would be for him the biggest mistake of all. For George W. Bush, the position is not an end in itself, but an instrument to accomplish an important mission—one rooted in the very fiber of his being.

History, in the end, will judge whether he got things done— and whether the *right* things got done *well*. There will be a long list of decisions to examine: the insistence on long-term tax cuts even as the long-term deficit swelled; the decision not to ask the nation for sacrifice in the war on terrorism; the strategy of elevating the threat posed by Iraq over al Qaeda's terrorism; the initial focus on Iraq over North Korea's nuclear weapons program; federal tax strategies that might have aggravated the budget problems in most state governments, which in turn proved a drag on the economy; and the decision to establish a huge new department of homeland security, with enormous startup costs that threatened to distract attention from the nation's core homeland security problems.

The judgment, of course, will depend on the values of those keeping score. At his core, Bush is a traditional, conservative, pro-business, antiregulation Republican. Those who don't share these values will quarrel with his record. His allies will celebrate his efforts to cement a new Republican majority around his core principles.

But it's hard to escape the basic fact that Bush has been successful in reshaping the fabric of public affairs. His genuine accomplishments are all the more remarkable because he so clearly overcame the fears—or hopes—of Americans that he was an amiable dunce. In fact, he has skillfully used this to considerable political advantage, by lowering expectations only to surpass them, time after time.

From his heart and from his core, Bush deeply believes that he knows what is best, for himself, for the nation, and for the world. From his experience, he had strong instincts about what would work. From his internal compass, he had a clear sense of what was right.

The ultimate challenge for Team Bush is making fine adjustments to that compass, honing the capacity to carry decisions out effectively—and to refining its vision against the harsh, shifting, risky realities of the 21st century world. He does not have a board of directors to confirm his judgment. In fact, as noted earlier, half of his board—the Democrats in Congress—are working to undermine his claim to power. Nor does he have a financial bottom line against which to assess his success.

Instead, he has a decision cycle that never stops and that sometimes accelerates. New problems relentlessly surface. Old problems doggedly reappear. Voters forget policy successes and pointedly ask, "What have you done for me lately?" His challenge is to spend his political capital to do the right thing, to do it well, and in the doing, to build more capital to broaden his base to pursue even more tests. It would be impossible to imagine a more challenging crucible in which to test Bush's style or his principles for leadership.

Sources and Notes

GEORGE W. BUSH HAS NEITHER written nor talked much about his management style. He does not spend much time in self-reflection. Whether he's running Oval Office meetings or frenetically clearing brush at his ranch, he is a man of action. As I wrote this book, there were few inside accounts of how the president managed the White House, and those accounts that did exist clearly had the stamp of individuals trying to spin the story to their own advantage.

That means the portrait of Bush's style has been woven together from a pastiche of interviews, campaign narratives, biographical portraits, and newspaper accounts. Bush's campaign autobiography, *A Charge to Keep* (New York: HarperCollins, 1999), is a revealing first-person account of the president's journey to the White House. But it also has some remarkable gaps. Bush, for example, devotes just a few pages to the tragic death of his sister when he was a young boy. He spends less than three pages on his days at the Harvard Business School. The book is filled more with a sense of his values—and where they come from—than on how he does his job. That itself is revealing about Bush and his style, since so much of his approach to Team Bush comes from the values that drive his life.

When Bush first launched his presidential campaign, *Texas Monthly* devoted the entire June 1999 issue to articles about Bush and his background. The magazine remains one of the most in-depth portraits of Bush before he moved to the White House, and vignettes from these articles continue to appear in newspaper stories.

For the Bush presidential years, the White House's Web site at www.whitehouse.gov is the foundation for research. It details Bush's speeches and comments, and its search engine is remarkably powerful. However, given Bush's penchant for malapropisms, the White House press office increasingly scrubbed the official version to ensure consistency in the message. Newspaper reporters delighted in finding and publishing more colorful versions than the official one, so press accounts have often provided useful supplemental portraits.

Texas's special brand of politics has also nourished an unusual breed of political journalist. Molly Ivins is surely one of the most lively, and her entertaining book, *Shrub: The Short but Happy Political Life of George W. Bush* (with Lou Dubose, New York: Vintage Books, 2000) is part keen political insight and part Texas rodeo. In *Ambling into History: The Unlikely Odyssey of George W. Bush*, *New York Times* reporter Frank Bruni captured his time traveling the campaign trail with candidate Bush. Together they help chart the road from Austin to the White House.

As useful as written sources are, there is nothing quite like watching the man in action. HBO's 2002 documentary, *Journeys with George*, is a fascinating film charting the Bush 2000 presidential campaign from its first days to victory. NBC News producer Alexandra Pelosi carried a video camera aboard the press campaign and caught remarkably fresh and uncensored moments of the candidate in action.

The film's first photography credit went to George W. Bush, who occasionally grabbed the camera and turned the tables on Pelosi and her fellow reporters. Bob Woodward's in-depth study of the way Bush waged the first months of the war against terrorism, *Bush at War* (New York: Simon and Schuster, 2002), provides an invaluable portrait of the president at work in some of the toughest and darkest days a president has faced in a generation. In *The Right Man: The Surprise Presidency of George W. Bush* (New York: Random House, 2003), David Frum provides a useful inside account as one of Bush's former speechwriters.

Understanding the way Team Bush works is one part Bush's style. But it's also two parts context. Bush is only the latest leader to confront the challenges of running the world's largest and most powerful organization, and understanding how his style and approach differs from other presidents is critical to my book's approach. Political scientists have explored these issues for years, and these books proved most useful in writing the book: Stephen Hess, *Organizing the Presidency*, 3rd ed. (Washington, DC: Brookings Institution Press, 2002); and Charles O. Jones, *Passages to the Presidency: From Campaigning to Governing* (Washington, DC: Brookings Institution Press, 1998). George Stephanopoulos's inside account of the Clinton administration, *All Too Human: A Political Education* (Boston: Little, Brown, 1999), provides a valuable base for comparison.

Whether watching films of candidate Bush or reading about him, one fact is clear. Even though Bush has worked at the center of an increasingly large and sophisticated apparatus, Bush himself has been remarkably the same man. The nation changed after September 11, but Bush did not. If anything, he became more of what he had already been: a leader who drew on his own sense of values to make strong, determined decisions. He built around him a team to help him do what he wanted to do, and that is the story of Team Bush.

BIRTH OF A COMMANDER IN CHIEF

"This stuff about transformed? ..." Anne E. Kornblut, "Year One: Faith, Resolve Steady Bush," *Boston Globe*, December 30, 2001, A1.

"never knowing when she might fall on her face." Robert Novak, "Advantage Bush," *CommentMax*, October 16, 2000, at http://www.newsmax.com/commentarchive.shtml?a=2000/10/16/093700

"Can nice guy George junior shed his image ..." BBC News, "Talking Point," August 15, 2000.

"It was, in fact, one of those moments ..." *New York Times,* September 12, 2001, A26.

"It's often said he's a man comfortable in his own skin ..." Vance McMahan, interview, December 3, 2002.

"The thing that struck me most ..." and subsequent discussion. Dick Kirschten, "Bush as Boss," *Government Executive*, July 2000.

"He was somebody who has as little degree of pretension ..." McMahan interview.

CHAPTER 1

"I wanted to be my own boss." George W. Bush, *A Charge to Keep*, New York: Harper Collins, 1999, 57.

"George spent a lot of time learning from other people...." Helen Thorpe, "Go East, Young Man," *Texas Monthly* June 1999.

"had become very serious ..." Michael Kranish, "Hallmarks of Bush Style Were Seen at Harvard," *Boston Globe*, December 28, 1999, A1.

"I wasn't political then." Kranish, *Boston Globe*.

"I am sure your Mr. Bush has all the amiable qualities you describe." From Molly Ivins and Lou Dubose, *Shrub: The Short but Happy Political Life of George W. Bush*, New York: Vintage Books, 2000, xxi.

"to know that [business] was *not* what I wanted to do with my life." Bush, *A Charge to Keep*, 57–60.

"Here you are at the West Point of capitalism." Bush, *A Charge to Keep*, 60.

"George was the person who in three months ..." Thorpe, *Texas Monthly*.

"I studied, and ran and rode my bike a lot." Bush, *A Charge to Keep*, 61.

"He was the perfect Sky Decker." John Solomon, "Bush, Harvard Business School and the Makings of a President," *New York Times*, June 18, 2000, Sec. 3, 17.

"wrote a decent essay." Kranish, *Boston Globe*.

"was not a star academic performer" and "was very good at getting along with people and getting things done." Solomon, "Bush, Harvard Business School and the Makings of a President."

"the motorcade was one car ..." Edwin Chen and Doyle McManus, "Valued Bush Confidant to Leave White House," *Los Angeles Times*, April 24, 2002, A1.

CHAPTER 2

"Every man who takes office in Washington ..." Attributed to Woodrow Wilson.

"he does have a strong belief in providence ..." ABC News, *Up Close*, December 20, 2002.

"Whenever you are asked if you can do a job ..." Attributed to Theodore Roosevelt.

"This is the only bureaucracy in Washington that can change to fit the personality of the president." Richard L. Berke, "Bush is Providing Corporate Model for White House," *New York Times*, March 11, 2001, Sec. 1, 1.

"Get me Knuckles on the line ..." Bruce McCall, "Yo, Sparky. Yeah, You Know Who You Are," *New York Times*, February 18, 2001, Sec. 4, 2.

Andrew Card's version of Bush's rules and Card's commentary. Berke, *New York Times*.

"I want justice." "Excerpts From Bush's Remarks on Retaliation," *New York Times*, September 18, 2001, Sec. B, 4.

"He'll sit here ..." Richard E. Neustadt, *Presidential Power: The Politics of Leadership*, New York: John Wiley and Sons, 1960, 9.

"Hidden-hand" presidency. Fred Greenstein, *The Hidden-Hand Presidency: Eisenhower as Leader*, New York: Basic Books, 1982.

"They ran their businesses according to a formula …" Henry Mintzberg and Joseph Lampel, "Do MBAs Make Better CEOs? Sorry Dubya, It Ain't Necessarily So," *Fortune*, February 19, 2001.

CHAPTER 3

"I'm not afraid to surround myself with strong and competent people." Stephen Hess, *Organizing the Presidency*, 3rd ed., Washington, DC: Brookings Institution, 2002, 168–169.

"Individual commitment to a team effort …" Attributed to Coach Vince Lombardi.

"I want a flat structure …" and "gave the senior staff members a great deal of access …" McMahon interview.

"did not want someone to be chief of staff who was over-territorial …" John P. Burke, "The Bush Transition in Historical Context," *PS: Political Science and Politics*, March 2002, 24.

"I hope the American people realize that a good executive …" Stephen H. Hess, *Organizing the Presidency*, 3rd ed. Washington, DC: Brookings Institution, 2002, 168–169.

"permanent campaign." Interview, September 20, 2002.

"Working in the White House should not be your first job." Charles O. Jones, *Passage to the Presidency*, Washington, DC: Brookings Institution, 1998, 106.

"Bush has tended to surround himself with people he's taken the measure of." Burke, "The Bush Transition in Historical Context," 25.

"Internal communications are in turmoil." McCall, *New York Times*, February 18, 2001.

"Bush speaks louder in body language than any politician I have ever seen" and "He is formidable in these informal settings." Paul Burka, "The W. Nobody Knows," *Texas Monthly*, June 1999.

"is to make sure you listen" and "If I have any genius or smarts ..." Bob Woodward, *Bush at War*, New York: Simon and Schuster, 2002, 74.

"One of my jobs is to be provocative ..." Woodward, *Bush at War*, 144.

"It was never clear how much he really knew ...," "This was always the rub with Bush ...," and "so vague and off-kilter it was almost wiggy." Frank Bruni, *Ambling into History: The Unlikely Odyssey of George W. Bush*, New York: HarperCollins, 2002, 240–241, 243.

CHAPTER 4

"They can say what they want about me ..." George W. Bush, speaking to NBC's Alexandra Pelosi, about fellow members of the media, *Journeys with George*, HBO documentary, 2002.

" ... people should do what they say they are going to do ..." Ronald Brownstein, "Bush's Agenda Strategy: First Stand Fast, Then Bend," *Los Angeles Times*, January 7, 2001, A1.

"Most White Houses are lucky if they get the furniture in." Richard L. Berke, "Bush's Transition Largely a Success, All Sides Suggest," *New York Times*, January 27, 2001, 1.

"No one in the public knew much who Ford was" and "but nobody every questioned his legitimacy." David S. Broder, "Bush's Challenge...," *Washington Post*, December 19, 2000, A39.

"half the voters thinking the president does not belong there ..." Broder, "Bush's Challenge."

"a presidency of small advances rather than broad, sweeping changes." Janet Hook, "The Presidential Transition: Deep Rift Awaits Bush in Capital," *Los Angeles Times*, December 15, 2000, A1.

"... to strike the right starting note." Berke, "Bush's Transition Largely a Success."

"Bush is a person who said what he believes." Brownstein, "Bush's Agenda Strategy."

"You lay out what your agenda is ..." Brownstein, "Bush's Agenda Strategy."

"At the end of the day, he knows what can pass and what can't pass." Brownstein, "Bush's Agenda Strategy."

"The Bush administration is following its own kind of Powell Doctrine ..." Franklin Foer, "After Meritocracy," *The New Republic*, February 5, 2001.

"wildcatter-in-chief." "More Oomph for Energy," *Business Week*, May 28, 2001.

"If the President is not careful ..." Richard S. Dunham, "Better Concentrate Real Hard, Mr. President," *Business Week*, June 4, 2001.

"I want him—I want justice." David E. Sanger, "Bin Laden Is Wanted in Attacks, 'Dead or Alive,' President Says," *New York Times*, September 18, 2001, A1.

"The Taliban must act ..." Elisabeth Bumiller, "Bush Pledges Attack on Afghanistan Unless it Surrenders Bin Laden Now; He Creates Cabinet Post for Security," *New York Times*, September 20, 2001, A1.

"This nation has defeated tyrants, liberated death camps ..." Elisabeth Bumiller, "Bush's Pilgrimage Ends with Vow to Prevail over 'Terrorist or Tyrant,'" *New York Times*, September 12, 2002, B8.

"The just demands of peace and security will be met ..." David E. Sanger and Elisabeth Bumiller, "Bush Presses U.N. to Act Quickly on Disarming Iraq," *New York Times*, September 13, 2002, A1.

CHAPTER 5
"I ... had the responsibility to show resolve. ..." Woodward, *Bush at War*, p. 96.

"He stays on message, and I think that really matters more than anything else. ..." Evan Smith, "How W. Can Lose," *Texas Monthly*, July 2000.

Number of presidential press conferences. Presidential scholar Martha Joynt Kumar, quoted in Jim Rutenberg, "White House Keeps a Grip on Its News," *New York Times*, October 14, 2002, C10.

"bumblebee" approach. Francine Kiefer, "To Ask Bush a Question, Wait Your Turn," *Christian Science Monitor*, April 6, 2001, 3. Kiefer was the "bumblebee" in question.

"has the uncanny ability to suck information out of a room." Jim Rutenberg, "White House Keeps a Grip on Its News," *New York Times*, October 14, 2002, C1.

"In this administration, the controls on information are tighter than in any other one I have covered." Rutenberg, "White House Keeps a Grip on Its News."

"to be very, very disciplined and treat the press like caged animals and only feed them on a regular schedule." Rutenberg, "White House Keeps a Grip on Its News."

"This is not an administration that's interested in a happy press. ..." Sridhar Pappu, "The Art of the Leak," *The New York Observer*, August 19, 2002, 1.

Sam Attlesey story on Bush's use of drugs. "Pumping Iron, Digging Gold, Pressing Flesh," *Newsweek*, November 20, 2000, 50–60.

"Wanted: Dead or Alive." Remarks by the President to employees at the Pentagon, September 17, 2001.

"They can run but they can't hide." The phrase was used in different combinations. See, for example, the president's remarks to U.S. Attorneys Conference, November 29, 2001.

"I told Karen it couldn't be done. ..." Gerson interview, *Up Close*.

"walks a high wire between the expectations he has raised ..." Ed Vulliamy, "Bush's Finest Hour," *The Observer*, September 23, 2001, *Observer* Special Supplement, 18.

"The president wants, in his speaking, action and directness ..." Gerson interview, *Up Close*.

"Enron is a much bigger story than anyone in Washington realizes." John Nichols, "Congress and War," *The Nation*, September 30, 2002, 4–5.

"If we meet our responsibilities, if we overcome this danger, we can arrive at a very different future." President's Remarks at the United Nations General Assembly, September 12, 2002.

"a clear message to corporate wrongdoers that handcuffs and a jail cell await those who violate the trust placed in them." Larry Neumeister, "Feds Arrest Adelphia Founder, Sons," *Pittsburgh Tribune-Review*, July 25, 2002.

"It should be clear to every shareholder, investor and employee in America ..." Radio Address by the President, July 27, 2002.

"One of the most dependable poll results is that people don't like polling." Joshua Green, "The Other War Room," *The Washington Monthly*, April 2002.

Washington Monthly survey of the administration's polling operations. Green, "The Other War Room."

"there's a lot more polling on spin." Green, "The Other War Room."

"the black arts of the Bush polling operation." Maureen Dowd, "Addiction to Addition," *New York Times*, April 3, 2002, A19.

CHAPTER 6

"... we don't have a lot of last-minute scrambling. ..." Gerson interview, *Up Close*.

"This is a buttoned-down administration, perhaps the most I've seen." Matthew Engel, "Bush Thrives on Crisis Management," *The [Manchester, UK] Guardian*, September 7, 2002, 4.

"I was so out of shape," along with the cover story. "A Postrun Chat with G.W.," *Runner's World*, October 2002.

"one of the saddest things about the presidency" and "it keeps me disciplined." *Runner's World*, October 2002.

"I guess that's part of the stress relief I get from it." Mike Allen, "Since Sept. 11, Exerciser Bush Finds Himself on War Footing," *The Washington Post*, August 22, 2002, p. A15.

Bush body fat measurements and pulse rate. Lawrence K. Altman, "Doctors Who Examine Bush Say He Is Exceptionally Fit," *New York Times*, August 7, 2002, A13.

"pump a few Arnies" and James Wilkinson pizza count. Dana Milbank, "Fit to Govern, and Then Some," *The Washington Post*, June 17, 2002, C1.

"The omnipresent feeling was confusion...." Joseph Curl, "Bush Runs on Time, Keeps Media and Staff Prompt," *Washington Times*, January 31, 2001, A1.

"How can we trust you? ..." and "I'm damn serious, pal. ..." Evan Smith, "George, Washington," *Texas Monthly*, June 1999.

"Political professionals look upon candidates as the baggage they have to carry on their way to being famous...." Smith, "George, Washington."

"NINA" administration—No Intellectuals Need Apply. Evan Thomas and John Barry, "Familiar Waters," *Newsweek*, January 8, 2001, 20–23.

"the White House is the only sieve that leaks from the top." Greg Pierce, "Inside Politics," *Washington Times*, January 21, 2002, A6.

"uninterrupted flood of damaging leaks...." Mark Shields, "Leak, Leak, Sink, Sink," *The Washington Post*, January 14, 1983, p. A15.

"I've had it up to my keister." Reginald Dale, "Reagan Orders Crackdown on Press Leaks," *The Financial Times [London]*, January 12, 1983, 4.

"anyone who talks out of turn doesn't last long." Engel, "Bush Thrives on Crisis Management."

Mike Parker story on congressional testimony. Francie Kiefer, "Backlash Grows Against White House Secrecy," *The Christian Science Monitor*, March 25, 2002, 3.

"The Bush loyalists have done an amazing job...." Byron York, "Leakproof?" *National Review*, 53 no. 19, October 1, 2001, 28–30.

"They run a button-up place." York, "Leakproof?"

Bush speed golf. Elizabeth Bumiller, "Bush Makes Quick Work of Relaxing," *New York Times*, August 5, 2002, A10.

CHAPTER 7

"George Bush and several talented people around him have made the White House a power center ..." Adam Nagourney, "Shift of Power to White House Reshapes Political Landscape," *New York Times*, December 22, 2002, Sec. 1, 1.

"In the past, those who foolishly sought power by riding on the back of the tiger ended up inside." John F. Kennedy, inaugural address, January 20, 1961.

Molly Ivins's description of Texas's "weak governor" system. Molly Ivins and Lou Dubose, *Shrub: The Short but Happy Political Life of George W. Bush* (New York: Vintage Books, 2000), xiii.

"to be for everything is to be for nothing." Burka, "The W. Nobody Knows."

"We had so many goals we had no goals." Vance McMahan interview.

"We envision a state where it continues to be true that what Texas can dream, Texans can do." *Vision Texas*, at http://www.tcb.state.tx.us/Strategic_Plan/Toc482673721.htm

"world-class schmoozer" and "He's the only governor I've ever known that I would like to have sitting on my back porch drinking beer and talking baseball." Edward Walsh, "Bush's Style Succeeded Even as Tax Plan Failed," *Washington Post*, November 25, 1999, A1.

The party once stood for "moderation, tolerance, fiscal responsibility." Jim Jeffords statement. *New York Times*, May 25, 2001, A20.

"It was less political hardball and more juvenile T-ball." David R. Guarino, "Card May Shoulder Blame for Departure," *Boston Herald*, May 25, 2001, 5.

"This administration has been stiff-arming Congress." Quoted by David Rogers, "Assertive President Engineers a Shift in Capital's Power," *Wall Street Journal*, October 22, 2002, A1.

"not since Richard Nixon stiffed the Congress during Watergate ..." *FindLaw* website, at http://writ.corporate .findlaw.com/dean/20020201.html

"This isn't about spending." Rogers, "Assertive President Engineers a Shift in Capital's Power."

"Any suggestion that the segregated past was acceptable or positive is offensive, and it is wrong." George W. Bush, statement at Philadelphia Marriott Hotel, December 12, 2002.

"something's going to have to change. This can't be the topic of conversation over the next week." Elisabeth Bumiller, "With Signals and Maneuvers, Bush Orchestrates an Ouster," *New York Times*, December 21, 2002, Sec. 1, 1.

"it was a clean extraction," "They've got a skilled surgeon coming in to run the Senate...," and "Whether you agree or disagree with this administration on policy..." Bumiller, "With Singals and Maneuvers, Bush Orchestrates an Ouster."

"Every time I bestow a vacant office I make a hundred discontented persons and one ingrate." Attributed to Louix XIV, by Voltaire, *Le Siècle de Louis XIV*, ch. 26.

"In time they all go native anyhow." Memo to Robert Reich, "'Lessons' for the Eleven Weeks," (August 13, 1992), from Charles O. Jones, ed., *Preparing to Be President: The Memos of Richard E. Neustad*, Washington, DC: AEI Press, 2000, 125.

"allows us to stay in the orientation and team-building business." Stephen Barr, "DubyaDubyaDubya.theRules," *Washington Post*, October 18, 2002, A35.

"We're all here to make a difference...." Results.gov, at http://www.results.gov/leadership/presidentmessage.html

"Governments should be results-oriented...." Statement in Philadelphia, PA, June 9, 2000.

"The scorecard employs a simple grading system common today in well-run businesses." Results.gov, at http://www.results.gov/agenda/scorecard.html

"President Bush's proposed Department of Homeland Security is an enormous grant of power to the executive branch...." CNN, go to http://www.cnn.com/2002/ALLPOLITICS/09/03/senate.homeland/

CHAPTER 8

"If I have erred, I err in company with Abraham Lincoln." Attributed to Theodore Roosevelt.

"My administration will continue to act on the lesson's we've learned so far ..." President Bush Signs 9-11 Commission Bill, November 27, 2002.

"Like certain distinctive wines, President George W. Bush does not travel well...." Ben Macintyre, "Until You Laugh at Plastic Fish, Bush Will Be a Mystery," *The [London] Times,* May 25, 2002, p. 26.

"has a lousy legal system," "Bush would be sitting in prison today," "The Americans have enough oil," and "Bush wants to distract attention from his domestic problems...." Peter Finn, "German Official Compares Bush on Iraq to Hitler," *Washington Post*, September 20, 2002, A19.

"If there is dissent within the administration, we never hear about it." Confidential interview with the author, November 12, 2002.

"He is *very* focused on what is and is not 'presidential level.' ..." and "He sniffs ill-conceived stuff by staff with almost unfailing intuition." Confidential interview with the author, October 7, 2002.

"Reaching out and embracing different perspectives..." Confidential interview with the author, November 6, 2002.

"All the incomprehensible maneuvering and circumvention does more than waste time..." Mitchell E. Daniels, Jr., "The Budget-Busting Habit Must End," *Washington Post*, June 5, 2001, A21.

"throwing the U.S. taxpayers' money," "doesn't seem brilliant to me," "He doesn't inspire much confidence," "He seems to put his foot in his mouth and stumble...," and "There are a lot of people who would like to see him gone in the next half hour." Jonathan Weisman, "Taking Stock of Paul O'Neill," *Washington Post*, July 18, 2002, E1.

"political piñata," Stephen Labaton, "Praise to Scorn: Mercurial Ride of S.E.C. Chief," *New York Times*, November 10, 2002, A1.

"The auditing of the auditors has been as reliable as the auditors themselves." "Three Regulators Gone," *Washington Post*, editorial, November 13, 2002, A26.

"a key advocate of my administration's agenda for growth, new jobs, and wider and more international trade." Bush statement on naming John Snow as Secretary of the Treasury, December 9, 2002.

"When I take action, I'm not going to fire a $2 million missile at a $10 empty tent and hit a camel in the butt." Dana Milbank, "At Crisis Time, A Motherlode of Bush Traits," *Washington Post*, September 6, 2002, A1.

"The government can offer no legal or practical excuse for excessive delay." Ellen Nakashima, "Bush View of Secrecy Is Stirring Frustration," *Washington Post*, March 3, 2002, A4.

"They seek to compel the vice president to give up documents..." Neely Tucker, "Cheney-GAO Showdown Goes to Court," *Washington Post*, September 28, 2002, A5.

CHAPTER 9

"I've got confidence in my capabilities. I love to be underestimated." "George W. Bush: Easy to Underestimate," *USA Today*, June 8, 2000.

"What we anticipate seldom occurs; what we least expected generally happens." Attributed to Benjamin Disraeli.

Not a bush but a "shrub." Molly Ivins and Lou Dubose, *Shrub: The Short but Happy Political Life of George W. Bush*, New York: Vintage Books, 2000.

"It makes it all the easier for President Bush to succeed." Richard S. Dunham, "The Best Way to Help Bush: Underestimate Him," *BusinessWeek Online*, January 29, 2001.

"I think we underestimate this man at our own peril." Dunham, "The Best Way to Help Bush."

"Those who think that they can say we're only going to have a stimulus package ..." Press conference, March 29, 2001.

"You come into office at zero years, and you've got 8 years ahead of you, hopefully." "A Life in Public Service," Conversations with Harry Kreisler, April 16, 1996 (Institute of International Studies, Berkeley, CA), at http://globetrotter. berkeley.edu/McNamara/mcnamara5.html

"My dad had earned enormous capital from the Gulf War ..." Walter Shapiro, "True Meaning of Election Can't Be Gleaned from Polls," November 6, 2002.

"It was as if everyone had underestimated him and by the time they wised up he was in control." Gregory Curtis, "How I Learned Not to Underestimate George W. Bush," *Time*, January 26, 2001.

"he and Rove went for broke." David S. Broder, "Political Steamroller," *Washington Post*, November 17, 2002, B7.

"O.K., he's not the brightest porch light on the block." Ivis and Dubose, *Shrub*, 194.

"To be effective is the job of the executive...." Peter F. Drucker, *The Effective Executive*, New York: HarperBusiness, 1967, 2002, 1.

Mary Matalin election estimate. CNN, at http://www.cnn.com/2002/fyi/news/11/05/elections/index.html.

"I would have crawled on broken glass." Elisabeth Bumiller, "Peace and Political Status at 39,000 Feet," *New York Times*, October 29, 2002, A24.

Estimate of Republican gains in state legislatures. Christopher Lee, "Republicans Make Historic Showing in Statehouses; GOP Realizes A Net Gain of About 200 Seats," *Washington Post*, November 7, 2002, A39.

"Bush was critical...." Tony Allen-Mills, "Barnstorming Bush on a Roll as Democrats Seek Saviour," *The Times* [London], November 10, 2002, 26.

"started with a narrow win in his first race for governor ..." Broder, "Political Steamroller."

"It was a 50-50 country before the election, and it's still a 50-50 country... I don't think this is an overwhelming mandate." Dana Milbank and Mike Allen, "White House Claims Election Is Broad Mandate," November 7, 2002, A27.

"It is a big victory." Milbank and Allen, "White House Claims Election Is Broad Mandate."

"The White House took a huge gamble; they rolled the dice, and it worked.... They won the 2000 election legitimately last night. He got his mandate, he got his victory and now he can govern for two years." Milbank and Allen, "White House Claims Election is Broad Mandate."

"He moves boldly even when he doesn't have any political capital.... He moves to create capital." Interview with the author, December 14, 2002.

"thinks the conventional wisdom about how you respond to a big victory is wrong.... It strengthens your hand to act." John Harwood, "New Appointments Show Bush Staying Conservative Course," *Wall Street Journal*, December 11, 2002, A4.

"We fight, as we always fight, for a just peace ..." The White House, *The National Security Strategy of the United States of America*, September 2002, 1.

"America is now threatened less by conquering states than we are by failing ones." The White House, *The National Security Strategy of the United States of America*, September 2002, 1.

"He's made a science out of selling tough partisan proposals with cool rhetoric." Mann interview.

"So much of politics and public life is chance and serendipity." Mann interview.

THE STRENGTH OF A LEADER

"... the executive is, first of all, expected to get the right things done." Peter Drucker, *The Effective Executive*, 1.

Index

Acknowledgments

THIS BOOK HAD ITS GENESIS in a series of conversations with Jeffrey Krames at McGraw-Hill. He raised the key questions: What is George W. Bush's style? How does it differ from the styles that other presidents have developed? Does it seem to work—for him and, just as importantly, for the country? The questions launched me down the winding road that ended in this book. I'm grateful indeed for his provocative suggestions and constant insights along the way.

The book benefited enormously from conversations and interviews with a great many people, including both Washington insiders and experts who have long followed presidential politics. I'm especially indebted to extended conversations with Charles O. Jones (University of Wisconsin-Madison), Thomas Mann (Brookings Institution), William Eggers (Deloitte Research and manager of the Texas Performance Review during Bush's governorship), and Vance McMahon (Bush's gubernatorial policy adviser). In addition, I interviewed a number of experts who spoke on background and requested anonymity. They immeasurably enriched the book.

Zachary Oberfield proved an untiring and unfailingly helpful researcher. He dug out important nuggets for the book—and he always proved a valued colleague in talking

219

through the issues raised by Bush's management style. He is a true professional in every respect.

McGraw-Hill's production staff was every author's dream. I'm especially indebted to Tom Lau, who designed the book's cover. He perfectly captured not only the Bush style but also the new blue-and-gold look that Bush brought to the Oval Office. Editing supervisor Scott Kurtz and production supervisor Maureen Harper flawlessly and painlessly managed the book's production. Likewise, Patty Wallenburg's typesetting was also exemplary and incredibly swift.

I owe the greatest debts to my parents—who taught me first and best about what teamwork really means—and to my wife, Sue. She not only provided unflagging support through the writing but also remarkably keen insight into how best to frame the book's themes. She is the best teammate an author (or husband) could ever have.

Donald F. Kettl